Fit, Fabulous and Focused How to Create the Life You Want After Forty

Fit, Fabulous and Focused
How to Create the Life
You Want After Forty

Yolanda Cornelius

FIRST EDITION

Printed in the United States of America

ISBN 13: 9780997406924
ISBN: 0997406925

Acknowledgements

would like to thank the special people in my life who helped make this project possible:

My Daddy, Allen, who promotes my book as a best seller even before I printed my first copy.

My boyfriend, Richard, who never interferes and always supports me as I chase my dreams.

My sisters, Cynthia and Broada, for making me laugh and keeping me grounded while I wrote this book.

My daughter, Khristah, for her love and support and giving me five adorable reasons (my grandkids) to stay motivated whenever I get writer's block.

Kristy @ We Party 2, for being my part-time T-shirt designer/party hostess/consultant. Thanks for all you do.

My cousin, Wanda, for constant encouragement, sharing and caring, and those Monday morning phone sessions.

My sidekick, Andrea H., who always helps me to see things from a different perspective. Thanks for listening my friend.

My crew, Mina, Valerie, Shawn and Andre who can find humor in ANY situation and always brighten my day. Nikki you do too!

My awesome editor, Melanie Saxton, for treating my manuscript like a Best Seller, understanding my vision and seeing it through to fruition.

Thanks to all of my coworkers and friends who encouraged me to keep going and reminded me often that I gave up cable television to write this book.

My Vision

A vision is an aspirational guide that helps identify what we want to achieve. One of our life goals should be to define our vision, and then unleash it.

My vision is as follows:

To utilize my talents to mentor, inspire, and empower women one goal at a time by:

- maximizing their full potential
- improving their health and wellness
- securing better financial positions
- developing their spiritual relationships
- nurturing personal relationships

I share this vision so that my readers who have reached the milestone of forty (and beyond) can develop their own version, personalized by their specific needs and goals. Consider the wisdom of the following quote by Marianne Williamson:

> "Our deepest fear is not that we are inadequate. Our deepest fear is that we are powerful beyond measure. We ask ourselves, who am I to be brilliant, gorgeous, talented, and fabulous? Actually, who are you not to be? You are a child of God. Your playing small does not serve the world. We were born to make manifest the glory of God that is within us. It is in everyone. As we let our own light shine, we unconsciously give other people permission to do the same."

I needed to read, hear and feel these words, for the sentiment awoke a fire inside of me as I journeyed toward becoming "Fit, Fabulous and Focused." While writing the pages of this book, I was reminded that life's challenges are simply opportunities in disguise, as described below:

I summoned my determination as a teenage mother to create a life of happiness for my daughter and me no matter the cost.

I channeled the confidence I displayed as a proud, newly decorated soldier marching across the parade fields in the United States Army.

I harvested the fearlessness I found within me as I renewed my business lease for a second and third time in the midst of personal hardships and financial uncertainty.

I reflected the radiance and resilience bestowed upon me as I became a grandmother in my thirties amongst critics and naysayers.

I renewed the faith within me that believes all things are possible through Christ who strengthens me.

~ Yolanda Cornelius

Who am I to be brilliant, gorgeous, talented and fabulous?
Actually, who am I not to be?

Dedication

To Team MiMi:
Kyla, Khamile, Antonio (AJ), Alex, and Steven III (Trent)

I hope I make you proud!

Love, MiMi

Table of Contents

Introduction

Yep, that's me driving in my car on I-85 North, heading to my new job in what seems to be the middle of nowhere, also known as Jefferson, GA. Population less than 10,000, no malls on the map, and plenty of open fields for my viewing pleasure. Although it's only two hours away, the closer I get to my destination, the more it feels like I'm a looonnngggg way from home. I'm a little bit nervous, somewhat uncertain, kind of anxious, and not quite happy, but I'm DEFINITELY determined to start fresh and see what this new adventure will bring.

Now before I share my innermost thoughts and let you in on this dynamic blueprint of how to create the life you want after forty, let me bring you up to speed on "WHY" I decided to do just that. It wasn't that my life before Jefferson was horrible by any means. I have the most loving and supportive family a Georgia girl could ask for. I'm very well connected in my hometown of Macon and have awesome friends, a fulfilling relationship with a wonderful man, and a great relationship with God.

In addition, my position with my previous employer was one that was literally created just for me by upper management. My salary afforded me a comfortable living as long as I lived within my means. I also previously owned a popular pole fitness studio in Macon (Diva Zone) with a loyal clientele in a great location.

There were definitely a lot of positive things going my way and I had already achieved several of the goals on my To Do/Bucket list by the age of forty. So with all of this positivity surrounding my life, what could possibly make me want to change it, and why on earth was I not satisfied? Why would I give up the stability of a government position, the security of being well-known and well-connected in my hometown, and the moderate success of a part-time business in order to move to the middle of nowhere with a bunch of complete strangers?

Was it unhappiness? Was it curiosity? Was it greed or selfish gain? No. It was something far more powerful and intense. It was my desire for GROWTH!

That's what happened. My desire for GROWTH became a force I could not ignore! It took over my thoughts, changed my behaviors, and led me to take action. It had been fifteen years since I moved back home to Macon to build a solid foundation for my daughter after leaving the US Army. Although I'd experienced a lot of bumps and bruises over those past fifteen years, I managed to find my comfort zone in Macon. I became complacent and settled for the status quo. You see, this was a great life to have, but it was no longer a great life for me.

Forty was a turning point. It was apparent that good ol' Macon could no longer offer what I needed, and the feeling of wanting something more than a "decent living" grew exponentially. This "tug" at my soul compelled me to take action, and that is "WHY" I decided to pack my bags and move to Jefferson.

I know there are lots of other women who are longing for growth. Believe me, ladies, there's no better season, time or reason than your fabulous forties (and beyond) to seize the moment and become Fit, Fabulous and Focused. So I thought, *Why not share my blueprint on how I created the life I wanted after forty?* You, too, can get motivated, get passionate, get energized or get fed up with your current status and create the life YOU want after forty.

You are under no obligation to be the same person you were a year, a month, or even 15 minutes ago.

You have the right to Grow.

No apologies.

Fit
(Awareness)

Now that you know "Why" I decided to create the life I wanted, let's talk about "How" I made it happen.

I didn't just wake up one day and decide to pursue my desire to grow. The notion simmered for years, especially in my thirties. Honestly, I thought about it all the time, but it wasn't until my forties that I actually figured out "How" to do it. I guess I was never quite motivated, frustrated, excited AND angry enough to follow through on my plans to make it happen... emphasis on AND—not OR. It wasn't enough for me to be really motivated OR very excited about creating the life I wanted. I could easily attend a Tony Robins seminar or watch an episode of Oprah's Life Class to achieve that. Likewise, if I wanted to be terribly frustrated or angry, I could simply show up for work and wait for my former boss to trigger the reaction.

Making the kind of change I desired required that all these emotions occur at the same time—a simultaneous mix of motivation, frustration, excitement AND anger—kind of like the Perfect Storm. This particular emotional storm could not be soothed by Keurig coffee fueled gossip sessions in my co-worker's offices. On-again, off-again participation in fitness boot camps and weekly pedicure indulgences could not relax me enough to melt away the frustration. It had gotten to a point where these feelings—this storm—would recur daily, sometimes more than once a day. I had become "aware" and I knew I had to start the process.

And so it began. Boom! Just like that, my compulsion to create the life I wanted became a reality. I was no longer talking about growth and change or daydreaming about it at the bookstore. I was making it happen. I just took action, and once I started I didn't second-guess my decision. Of course I would be lying if I said it was smooth sailing from that point on and everything went according to plan. Who am I kidding? I didn't even have a plan. I just took action. No game plan, no playbook, just action. The bottom line was that I was finally on my way toward becoming mentally and emotionally "Fit"—the first equation in the formula of "Fit, Fabulous and Focused."

So there you have it in a nutshell, the all-important "How." Getting to this point wasn't easy and I made a few mistakes along the way. Thankfully, the trailblazing effort culminated into a blueprint that can definitely help you successfully create your very own Fit, Fabulous, and Focused experience.

Let's get started, shall we?

CHAPTER 1

Motivate Yourself. Stop Making Excuses

Soon after my journey began, I discovered the hard truth about real change. In order to become mentally "FIT," we have to deal with a few personal emotional hurdles called "self-defeating" behaviors (SDBs). These SDBs are also known as procrastination, doubt, fear, laziness, stress, inability to say no, lack of discipline, and guilt, just to name a few. Sound familiar?

If we want to create a better life for ourselves, these behaviors have to be conquered. Only then are we emotionally prepared to get our heads in the game. For me personally, it was past time to seriously address my mental fitness. The word "FIT" in this self-help guide is not only about getting physically fit (as you will read about in chapter 2), but involves becoming emotionally prepared for what is yet to come.

Getting FIT is a stage of awareness. It's the stage where you begin to see things differently and question your own behaviors. Getting FIT is when you begin to take ownership of your destiny.

Initially, I thought the process of getting mentally "FIT" would be emotionally draining, but surprisingly that wasn't the case. The 30-day challenges provided at the end of each chapter and throughout this guide helped me keep the process exciting and stimulating, and will do the same for you. These challenges are powerful tools that help develop new habits and help you break old ones—forever!

News and Noise

Do you find yourself tuning in to multiple stations all repeating the same news throughout the day? If you are like me, you are probably hoping to get the "scoop." Funny thing is, once I got the scoop I had no one to tell. Everyone in my social media circle already knew the same scoop! Obviously, I wasted a lot of time collecting redundant information and this revelation prompted me to delete icons like Yahoo on my cellphone. Once I removed those apps and cleared the search history on my computer, it was a whole lot easier to stop obsessing over the news. I was no longer a slave to CNN.com, and I also suspended "some" of my social media accounts. This helped me curb the excessive surfing and clicking.

As for cable TV, I didn't realize how much time I squandered lying on the couch and binge-watching Law and Order and Criminal Minds, especially on weekends. I was even glued to re-runs, as if the ending would change since the last time I watched. My semi-addictive television habit was nothing more than a mind-numbing distraction. It had to be curbed, so I got rid of cable, as well. These "sacrifices" may seem small to you, but cutting the useless "noise" out of my daily routine had a profound impact. I gained back the precious hours needed to undertake my new journey. It allowed me to focus on what was truly important.

In hindsight, perhaps my news and cable addiction was simply a way to fill a void. I know now that these online activities were a barrier to "growth." Sure, they kept me busy, but the busy-ness was unhealthy. In fact, they masked a void in my social life. You see, most of my friends commuted in from bigger cities, so there were very few opportunities to hang out after work. To make matters worse, living in the middle of nowhere created a serious lack of leisurely activities. So after significantly reducing my online footprint, I found myself puttering around my apartment to stave off boredom, all the while concocting a recipe for "getting motivated." Soon, I was able to draw on the "Perfect Storm" of emotional frustration and take charge of the free time I had after work.

I seized the opportunity to develop short-term and long-term goals. It became the official kick-off in my journey towards becoming Fit, Fabulous and Focused. I bought a calendar and began writing down each goal. I also formulated plans to achieve them. For instance, I made a commitment to finish my book—not my usual verbal commitment, but an actual written commitment with deadlines and a timeline. Then I took action to meet those deadlines by setting a daily alarm on my phone for structured times to work on the manuscript.

Self-motivation comes in many forms. For me, posting individual sticky notes of my personal and professional goals in the middle of my bathroom mirror helped me renew my commitment every morning and every night. And I literally got off the couch! I created a dedicated workspace in my living room and pushed the front of my couch against the wall to prevent myself from sitting there and wasting time. As I entered my apartment daily, sitting on my couch was no longer a temptation. The silver lining was that it prompted me to join a gym and interact with real live human beings! Slowly but surely, I began to experience a transformation unlike any other.

However, getting off the couch may not be an easy option in your household. You may have others to consider. You may be single, divorced, or married to a partner who doesn't help out, or struggling financially, or stuck in a dead-end job... and this requires some creative thinking as you tackle your goals. The key is to strategically tailor your commitment based on your current situation. Even if you are caring for a loved one or feel overwhelmed, you can no longer allow yourself to use those reasons as excuses. You must draw upon your own "Perfect Storm" and take charge. You must get motivated and make plans that fit your circumstances.

I know this from personal experience. I also know the change you seek starts from within. So no more digital "noise," no more couch dependency, and no more excuses!

Now What?

Now you've embraced the concept of balancing your needs and the needs of your household. This means it's time to take action—the key to this whole process. Getting motivated is the "easy" part because it draws on your "Perfect Storm" of feelings and emotions. But the real question is, *Will you actually take the next step and make plans, set goals and achieve them?* That's the hard part. It requires a pinch of gumption and quite a bit of fortitude.

But taking action doesn't always happen over night. Sometimes you must make several passes around the same block before you are motivated enough to choose a different route. I experienced this back in 2006 after returning to work the week after my mother's funeral. My General Manager asked me to either resign or step down to a lower position within the company. He explained that my performance had been less than stellar for the past few months and that they were hiring someone else to fill my role. I didn't see that coming and wanted to scream, "Are you freaking kidding me?" I had just spent the last eighteen months watching my mom die slowly during an agonizing battle with colon cancer...and they wanted to talk about my job performance? *Seriously?*

I couldn't afford the pay cut that came along with a demotion. Honestly, I felt like kicking my boss in the balls and walking out. But I decided to resign from my position gracefully. Losing my job really bothered me. I didn't like feeling helpless, but I didn't have time to properly process my feelings because I needed another job ASAP.

So I made a few phone calls, and as fate would have it I found another accounting position within thirty days. It felt like I had things under control and my confidence returned. But after about a year and a half things became financially unstable at the company. By the end of 2007, the owner closed the business. Once again I was out of a job, but the stakes were higher this time. I had just recently signed a one-year lease for the new location of my Pole Fitness studio. Now I was deeply in debt and had no real income. My studio had only been open for one month and was not yet generating revenue. I was now panicking because so much was on the line.

Thankfully, when I learned about my employer's financial hardships earlier that year, I followed my gut instinct and sent out resumes. Yes, I was proactive, but this was a far cry from being motivated enough to step outside of my comfort zone. I simply wanted to find another job—a robotic reaction to unemployment, complete with status quo rationale. Within the same week I was hired as an accountant at a larger, more established company...or so I thought. I worked in this position for about five months, until one beautiful sunny morning when my world crashed in again. It could not have been a more beautiful day, which was ruined when the CEO/President of the company called and said, "Please let the employees know that we are no longer open for business."

My General Manager and I were shocked, but assumed it was only temporary. It wasn't. The CEO announced, "We will not reopen. We are closing our doors permanently." He didn't even bother to stop by and explain why. I spent the rest of that morning scrambling to pay the employees one final time, and tried to field their questions without having real answers. Just like that, my job was gone for the third time in a two-year span! It was a punch to the gut! I was totally stressed without a clue about what to do next, because this time I had no warning that my employer was in financial trouble!

I remember thinking, *Okay God, what is going on? What are you trying to tell me? Did I make the wrong move by opening my studio? Are you mad at me? Why does this keep happening?*

This time around, I let the "Perfect Storm" work its magic. I was finally motivated enough to wrestle control away from Corporate America and break a cycle that kept repeating itself. After all, I couldn't keep making the same moves and expect a different result—that's the definition of insanity! So after taking a day to process all that happened, I decided not to look for a full-time job. Instead I contacted a local temp agency and signed up for contract accounting positions to keep my income flowing. This gave me time to think, as well as some wiggle room to plan my next move. Soon I was walking a brand new path by deciding to focus on my pole fitness studio. I was intent on building my own business and future. Yes, it was still worrisome, but I was taking action in a new direction! I was growing!

Would you like to grow, too? The ideas below can help you achieve your goals by working "smarter" rather than "harder." These concepts can nudge you in directions you never thought possible. That's what being "Fit, Fabulous and Focused" is all about.

Be Productive

Yeah, I know. You're tired and had a long day. We all have long days and even longer weeks from time to time. But sitting on the couch for hours won't make your days any shorter. And it certainly won't make your days more productive. When you get home, avoid the couch and keep it moving! After all, if you work in an office environment, chances are you've already sat for several hours that day.

Think of it this way: our bodies are wonderfully designed to move. When God created us, he included muscles, cartilage and bone so that we could flex, bend, stretch, lift and reach. He primed us for productivity, both mentally and physically. We are meant to move. We are designed to be productive. Although man invented the couch, we were not designed to become couch potatoes.

However, there are special circumstances that earn some well-deserved "couch" time. If your job is physically demanding or labor intensive, then you'll probably want to relax and unwind. By all means, do so. I am not encouraging you to deny your mind and body the rest it needs, but once you are mentally and physically replenished you should immediately get back to planning and preparing your next move. Try going on a walk to refresh your mind.

The bottom line is that setting limits to your couch time is a positive life skill. It keeps your resting periods from becoming stagnation periods. Get out your To Do list and turn off the TV. Leave your cellphone in your purse (out of sight, out of mind)— but keep the volume on high so that you won't miss important calls. We must embrace the fact that television and cellphones are both major distractions that prolong our time on the couch, feeding a vicious cycle. Break that cycle! If your lifestyle permits, shut off any distraction possible to ensure optimum productivity.

Manufacture Motivation

Ever heard of the saying, "Fake It 'till you feel it?" Well, that slogan not only applies to boosting your self-confidence, but also applies to getting motivated. It would be the ideal scenario if everyone was automatically programmed with enough emotion, passion and opportunity to take action and achieve their goals. Unfortunately, life doesn't work that way.

In reality, we all have to make it happen, whether we want to or not. Every day we "manufacture motivation" to accomplish things that don't interest us at all. You may not want to cut the cucumbers for your salad, but you do it anyway because you are trying to eat healthier. You may not relish the thought of writing briefs, finishing projects, attending meetings, or managing budgets, but you do it anyway because it's your job and you take pride in your work. It may be tempting to lay on the couch and enjoy cake, but your mind, body and spirit deserve so much more. So we "conjure up" the motivation to do what needs to be done at work and on the home front, like it or not.

Manufacturing our own motivation can also be fun! For example, you may have a burning desire to lose weight and get in shape. The problem is, you love to eat and hate to exercise. So what do you do? You manufacture a little motivation to get the ball rolling. You can motivate yourself through the power of small rewards. Keep it simple. Every thirty days, reward yourself with a small token, like a pedicure for successfully working out four days a week. Maybe you can buy yourself a new outfit or new athletic gear every time you lose ten pounds. The objective is to make the reward small but enticing, and the goal challenging yet achievable, within a specific period of time.

We all need doses of optimism, and yes, you can manufacture that too! Tell yourself positive things even when you don't feel like it. Smile when you feel there is nothing to smile about. You may have to plaster your mirror with positive affirmations and change the screen saver on your computer to an inspirational quote. These little reminders will help keep you motivated and on track. They will become your mental springboard on days when you have to leap over the hurdles. Your daily affirmations will help you defeat procrastination, fear, uncertainty, doubt and even plain ol' laziness. Finding ways to manufacture motivation is crucial as you tackle the tough times and move forward.

Find Inspiration

Inspiration is an essential ingredient that helps push onward. It sustains your momentum, and without it you may never reach your goals. So do whatever it takes to find inspiration. Watch a movie with a powerful message. Update your To-Do List. Download a motivational musical play list on your iPod. Watch inspirational You Tube videos. Toot your own horn every now and then on social media. Get rid of clutter in your life and create a space for new projects.

There are a million ways to get inspired and rise above your current circumstances. Make a vision board or a vision book with details. Spend time every day envisioning yourself as someone who has achieved her goals. Reconnect with someone who has positively influenced you in the past. Emulate someone who is a mover and shaker. Shadow someone in a higher position and make them your mentor. Take yourself to dinner. Start a dreams and goals journal. Meditate, travel to a new city, have a brainstorming session, attend a women's retreat, or take a day off from work and do something impromptu like attend a networking function. Meet new people and let others learn from you, as well.

Where else can you find inspiration? How about right at home! Try a new recipe. Have sex in a different room or role-play with your partner. Call your Bestie and give yourself a before and after makeover. Read daily devotionals. Read the Bible. And when you feel like venturing out, visit a comedy club. Ask someone of another ethnicity on a date. Buy yourself something nice (but affordable) and update your wardrobe. Take a continuing education class at a local college. Consider donating your time to a community service project. Pay it forward. Do random acts of kindness—and don't tell the world about it on Facebook. Let your good deeds be their own reward.

Positive peer pressure is a great way to receive and share encouragement, so become inspired by the positivity of others. We are social creatures and enjoy interaction. The benefits are mutual, because many people have walked in your shoes and will likely weigh in with words of encouragement. So as you motivate them, they will motivate you—a win/win dynamic!

You can find inspiration everywhere! Just open your mind, unlock your heart, and keep looking!

Create Excitement

Let's say you have a new project and want to build excitement. Don't just talk about it. Plan your excitement! This will add momentum to your efforts, especially if you are starting your own business, changing career fields, or chasing personal dreams.

Develop some buzz and get others involved. Create a social media page and post blurbs about your day-to-day experiences. If you have a new product line or new service, stir up some interest by sending email blasts with incentives such as coupons or free samples. Build anticipation by sharing subtle hints and repeatedly post the launch date. Talk up your service or product on a blog. Contact online deal websites like Groupon or Living Social and offer discounted rates to new customers. Incorporate other resources such as joining a networking group and collaborating with others who have similar interests. Offer to be a guest speaker at a marketing event.

If you are starting a lengthy personal project like building a new home or remodeling a room, post pictures of the work progress. People love following these stages of development and will give you feedback. Likewise, if you're trying to lose weight, stop smoking, or live a healthier lifestyle, why not start a "Fitness with Friends" group or join a specialized support group? There is strength in numbers, so surround yourself with likeminded adventurers. Get advice from others who have already achieved similar goals. Post a group goal within your peer group and commit to it publicly, because group goals promote encouragement and often increase the level of commitment amongst your peers.

Share a few of your deadlines or significant dates on your timeline with your trustworthy inner circle. It may help to have others that you trust to hold you accountable and give you additional encouragement. Track each other's progress. Share your wins, your losses and your challenges while creating a game plan to ensure that you reach the next milestone on your timeline.

Last but not least, perhaps you're relocating to a new city, changing jobs, or getting married. You can ramp up the excitement by sharing special moments with friends and family. Send or post pictures. Use Face time, Glide and Skype to connect in real time and make the excitement contagious. Even something as mundane as a new diet or fitness routine can excite others. Allow them to celebrate with you! Authentic and hard-earned "good news" can uplift and motivate your peers, family and friends.

In short, this world is often too focused on the negatives. It is easy to forget that life is filled with wonder—and wonderful people. There's so much to be excited about. If you ever need a reminder, jot this quote on a Post It note and leave it on your mirror:

"Enthusiasm is excitement with inspiration,
motivation, and a pinch of creativity."
~BO BENNETT

Modify Your Daily Routine

Have you ever found yourself stuck in a rut? Truthfully, we all can get bogged down in the daily minutia. This is why modifying our routines is so important.

This modification effort isn't about changing our route as we drive home from work or choosing a different day to grocery shop. This particular type of modification is about changing our daily routines to produce a different outcome—a BETTER outcome. It's time to reevaluate our routines when we pursue our daily tasks with such vigilance that we don't even recognize the rut we've created!

For instance, are you fixated on becoming more efficient? Is it your goal to become faster at day-to-day tasks? If so, be careful not to sacrifice quantity for quality. Being motivated does not mean we should find new ways to cram more tasks into our day. The right motivation creates opportunities to achieve your goals without creating chaos. You want to be free from the rut, so compounding it defeats the purpose. Right?

There is a better way to operate—a way that allows you to "work smarter." Take a moment to assess your daily agenda and make small but noticeable changes in your routine. Instead of hitting the treadmill at the gym at 5:30 every day, try meeting up with a friend at the local track and power walk for a few laps. You can still achieve your fitness goal, but with the added motivation of fresh air, good conversation and the change in scenery. Rather than cooking for your family as a part of your "wifely duties," try choosing a family-friendly recipe that involves everyone in meal preparation. It creates family bonding time, but also ensures your loved ones appreciate the work that goes into preparing dinner. You can also opt for my personal favorite and choose a meal that you and your partner can cook together. It will spark lots of conversation and provides ample foreplay and motivation to "spice up" your love life.

Here's a tip that can immediately lighten your load. Take your routine modification a step further by eliminating non-essential tasks. If you've been following a regimented schedule for a period of time, then challenge yourself to reduce or "unschedule" the unimportant tasks. Try asking yourself the following questions:

- Will the task you are working on help you to achieve your current goal?
- Does it add value to or improve your current or future state of being?
- Is it a task you can delegate?

- Is this task still relevant or necessary to achieve the outcome you want?

Once you answer the questions above, take a second and even a third look at your current daily routine. Then take action to eliminate those tasks that are non-essential. By decluttering your schedule, you are actually decluttering your life. You'll find that you have more time in your day and are motivated to focus on the things you love to do.

Focus on One Goal at a Time

Setting too many goals at once, failing to prioritize, shuffling a lot of distractions, and multitasking can throw your mental state into overload. It dampens motivation, which is the exact opposite of what you want to accomplish. When too much is going on at one time, it's easy to lose focus, and even easier to flounder.

Try sticking to one main goal and work towards it daily. Break large tasks into smaller chunks and prioritize those chunks by order of importance. Create block schedules for your personal time and only focus on a specific task during each block. Block scheduling can be used whether you are an entrepreneur or someone who works a regular 9 to 5 job. For example, open and respond to emails between the hours of 8am and 10am. Set meetings with clients or run errands between 10am and 1pm. Work on projects after lunch between 2pm to 5pm. If you have limited control of your schedule on your job and cannot set block schedules during business hours, then utilize this concept with your time after work and on weekends.

Of course there is nothing wrong with having multiple goals. You will more than likely have more than one goal in your lifetime. But remember, the key to successfully completing those goals is to pursue them individually so that you don't become overwhelmed. After all, bite-sized morsels are much easier to digest one at a time.

Think Benefits—Not Obstacles

Perhaps some of the ideas above have left you wanting more! The last concept of this chapter prompts us to think about "benefits" rather than "obstacles" as we strive to accomplish our goals. No doubt, there will be times you will have to scale some hurdles before you can complete a goal, but the effort takes you to the next level in your journey. Sometimes the only way to motivate yourself is to focus solely on the benefits instead of the obstacles.

Make time each day to think about the positive aspects of whatever your new endeavor may be. Do you struggle with time management? Thankfully, there's a tweak for that! Are you feeling overwhelmed? You can tweak that too! A few positive "life tweaks" will get you back on course. For instance, your lunch and break periods will be far more productive if you avoid social media, music and office gossip. Instead, use this valuable time to take a walk and enjoy the great outdoors. Count your blessings and enjoy the weather. If it's raining, walk a few flights of stairs. These activities will clear your head and help you focus on your objective, which is to be mentally and physically fit. These solitary moments are also a great time to pat yourself on the back for keeping your goals in focus! See? You've just uncovered some hidden benefits by ignoring the obstacles.

Have you heard of journaling? It's a wonderful way to help sort your emotions, increase self-awareness, and track your accomplishments. You'll enjoy an abbreviated form of journaling by simply jotting down the new benefits you experience daily. Grab a pen and a notepad and become your own scribe, your own author, and the keeper of your own truth. As you think of a new benefit, write it down. Are you feeling more powerful and in control of your life? Write it down! Are you proud of your determination? Write it down! Are you staying on task and making better use of your time? Write it down! Capture the benefits on paper and make it your testimony. Don't procrastinate, because as the day progresses it's tempting to forget the benefits and focus on the obstacles.

Getting motivated can be tough, especially if you've been in a slump for a while. Perhaps you need a jumpstart in the form of inspirational "challenges"—just the sort of thing to get your motor running. "Dare" yourself with one or more of the following motivational challenges. You can track them in your mini journal too!

30-Day Motivational Challenges

I'm happy to recommend some tried-and-true formulas that will help get your head back in the game. Try one or all of these 30-day challenges and you'll be up and moving in no time!

Become a Morning Person 30-Day Challenge:

- Set your clock to wake up 30 minutes to one hour earlier than usual.
- Go to bed earlier than your usual time. Try 9:30 or 10:00pm.
- Don't press snooze. Get up when the alarm rings the first time.

Minimize Distractions 30-Day Challenge (Take a "Media Fast"):

- Give up TV and stop following the news.
- Don't use the Internet for anything virtual for 30 days. No online banking, no social media, no Pandora, no You Tube, no CNN, no Netflix, or Hulu for 30 days.
- Check your email once per day unless it's work related.

Prioritize Your Goals 30-Day Challenge:

- Write at least one goal you'd like to accomplish on a piece of paper within the next 30 days. It can be personal or professional.
- Stick your goal on the mirror and say it out loud every morning when you wake up and every night before bed for the next 30 days.
- Dedicate at least 45 (uninterrupted) minutes per day to an activity that will help you achieve your goal.

30-Day Breakfast Challenge:

- Eat a nutritious breakfast every day for 30 days.
- Avoid doughnuts and other pastries for breakfast.
- Don't consume coffee and sodas as a supplement for a nutritional breakfast.

Initially, you may feel you don't have time in your day to make this happen. But you will find the time, thanks to your new routine. Then one day in the not-so-distant future you'll look back at this journey and see the growth. You'll see a Fit, Fabulous and Focused new YOU staring back from the mirror.

CHAPTER 2

Find a Workout You Love

Now that we've covered mental fitness, it's time to address physical fitness. People who are both mentally and physically fit are less prone to health issues and generally live life to the fullest.

Personally, I've never been a traditional fitness regimen kind of girl. You know, going to the gym, running three to five miles a day, and pumping iron. After serving eight years in the US Army in my twenties and having to do physical training five days a week, I assumed I would somehow become fond of traditional fitness. Unfortunately, I didn't.

Honestly, there has been NO other form of exercise that makes me come alive like pole fitness. That may surprise you, and at first it surprised me! I had no clue that this sexy and powerful kind of workout would make me feel motivated, intrigued, and excited at the same time. I adore it so much that I opened up my own pole fitness studio. It was extremely fulfilling to watch the transformation in the lives of my students, not to mention the satisfaction of developing a business plan and making it happen.

But moving to a new city meant that I had to close my fitness studio. To fill the void I joined a gym, took yoga classes and participated in fitness boot camps to help me stay in shape. After about eight months of following this regimen, I reaffirmed that I really hate running, yoga puts me to sleep, and going to the gym is still one of my least favorite things to do. In short, nothing came close to pole fitness.

By now you're probably wondering how I found and fell in love with pole fitness. After all, this type of workout has been over-stereotyped as "something done by strippers in gentlemen's clubs." Well, thanks to a good friend named Lisa, I learned the facts. Pole fitness is a blend of artistry and exercise that works every muscle in your body. No matter your body type, level of fitness, or age, spinning on a pole is a mesmerizing and rewarding way to become Fit, Fabulous and Focused.

My interest was piqued when Lisa called me after taking her first pole dancing lesson. She was beyond ecstatic about the experience and could hardly tell the story! I clung to every word as she described what it was like in her first pole class. She gave intimate details on the spins, the music, and the instructor's techniques, and spoke enthusiastically about going to purchase her first pair of clear heel shoes! As she described every moment of the class in an almost orgasmic manner, I got excited too! I think I screamed. I think we both did.

By the end of our conversation, I had caught pole fitness fever and knew I had to try the class for myself. Lisa spoke of the confidence and motivation she felt, so I booked my session with anticipation. But it took a few weeks to get in due to the popularity of pole dancing! So I anxiously waited for the day to arrive, and it finally happened. I was on my way to my first pole class.

After an hour's drive on a Wednesday night, I arrived at a small lingerie boutique in Decatur. The instructor was in the process of securing a proper studio, but in the meantime classes were offered at the lingerie boutique to meet the high level of demand. It didn't matter that the parking lot had potholes jagged enough to blow out all my tires. I didn't care about the commute or anything other than the excitement Lisa described during her phone call.

Inside the boutique were two poles and three instructors. I nervously waited in line with about 15 other women until it was my turn to spin. Even though some of the ladies had taken the class before, we were all still giddy with excitement like school girls at a high school football game. Finally I reached the front of the line and stood next to the pole. The instructor stood a few feet away and gave me the signal. I grabbed the pole with both hands, closed my eyes, and flung my body around the pole as hard as I could.

After several exhilarating rotations, my spin came to an end and I opened my eyes. I couldn't believe it. I did it. I really did it and it was AWESOME! I took a deep breath, stood up straight, and reluctantly let go of the pole. Then I walked to the back of the line to await my turn again, barely managing to suppress the overwhelming desire to throw my hands to the sky and yell "SUPERSTAR."

My spin may have only lasted for five seconds, but those seconds made the impression of a lifetime. It was everything Lisa described, and more. I remember thinking on my drive back home, "Damn, I have got to do this again." I felt so empowered—all that was missing was my cape!

The next day I woke up with incredibly sore arms and obliques that ached like crazy, but all I could do was lay there and smile. I reminisced about my class for the rest of the day and was determined to learn everything about this new fitness endeavor. Soon I was a dedicated student of Aerial Inverts, Transition up, Bendy Diva and Bridged Outside Leg Hang. I became an expert at more daring moves like the Nose Breaker Drop, Cocoon, La Roue and Dangerous Bird. From beginner to extreme levels, pole fitness has something for everyone and merges the disciplines of dance and calisthenics, with a dose of exotic flair.

I had found and fell in love with the perfect workout! When I realized that many women would welcome an edgy and creative way to get in shape, I decided to open my own studio and share the love. Now it's time for YOU to find a workout you love, whether it be pole fitness or any of the ideas below.

Be Creative

Who says that you have to play by the rules when it comes to finding a workout that's right for you? Every woman is different. You deserve a regimen that sparks your interest and keeps you coming back for more!

If you don't have a friend in your life like Lisa, try channel surfing, especially if you have difficulty falling asleep late at night. Just turn on your television and check out a few alternative fitness infomercials. Likewise, if you find yourself in bed on a Saturday morning, Google adventurous forms of exercise. There's a world of workout options to choose from. One (or even more) of those options can help you achieve your fitness goals.

For instance, if you have a busy on-the-go lifestyle, perhaps you'll like Shaun T's T25 workout. This twenty five minute intense full body workout is for people who can't spend an hour in the gym every day. There are also the Beach Body 10-Minute Trainer workouts for those of us are just looking for a quick way to get in shape and stay healthy. Both workouts can be done from the comfort of your own home, on your schedule, and without expensive unused gym memberships.

If you want to add a little more intensity to your workout, try the P90X or the Insanity workout DVD series. Both of these workouts require intense discipline and total commitment to achieve your desired results. The P90X program is a 90-day program that combines strength training, cardio, martial arts and yoga. The workouts are usually one hour a day for six days a week. Insanity is a 60-day program that combines total body workouts based on cardio and circuit training. This is known as max interval training. You train your body as hard as possible for 3 minutes and take 30 second rest periods in between. Insanity routines are 30 and 60 minutes in length, six days a week.

But not all of the alternative workouts require intensity and strict discipline. Workouts like Cize, Hip-Hop Abs and the Country Heat Dance Workout focus on low-impact, high-energy dance moves. These choreographed cardio workouts are designed to help you break a sweat and burn lots of calories. Dance workouts may require a little more rhythm than the ones mentioned earlier, but they can also be done in the comfort of your home, as well. There's even a work out for avid television watchers called the Commercial Break Workout (also known as the Couch Potato Workout). It includes quick exercises you can do during the commercial breaks of your favorite TV shows.

And we can't mention home-based exercise without discussing Wii Fitness! Nintendo users have enjoyed Wii games for years, which explains the popularity of golf, tennis, bowling, baseball, and boxing for all ages! Entire families work out to these games, but they are also great for individuals. Wii offers exercise and nutrition programs as well, so it's definitely an investment to consider.

If you don't have a hectic schedule or a love-hate relationship with the gym as I do, you can venture out to your local fitness center and check out their daily schedule of alternative fitness workouts. Perhaps you have a clubhouse in your neighborhood, or a recreational park with full amenities, or a nearby YMCA. Yoga, Spin classes, and Zumba are popular favorites on most fitness center workout schedules.

When it comes to Yoga, I had no idea of the physical and mental benefits of this ancient practice. It's been around for decades and has become the preferred way to relax and release your tensions, but is also a great way to incorporate flexibility, stretching, balance and coordination into your workout routine. This Hindu spiritual discipline helps with breath control, meditation, and body posture. Traditional yoga styles such as Hatha and Vinyasa are widely recognized and taught at local gyms and fitness centers. Hatha is most popular with beginners because it's taught at a slower pace. You can also find more advanced yoga classes like Bikram and Hot Yoga at studios in your area. And if you are a real yoga buff, you may even want to try aerial yoga.

If achieving Zen and mastering your Chi is not your forte, perhaps you can try a more upbeat workout. Zumba, for instance, combines aerobic fitness with Latin American dance. At one point Zumba classes were spreading like wildfire, and they remain highly popular. The low cost, one-day certification process for Zumba instructors and the initial $6 price point of a Zumba class created a win-win situation for instructors and their clients. These classes quickly became the premier fitness alternative for women nationwide. Because of its non-threatening approach and quick results, classes are offered in almost any setting with an open space and good lighting, including churches and corporate offices.

My next fitness endeavor will be a spin class. This involves indoor cycling classes that mix endurance, strength, intervals, high intensity (race days) and recovery. Spin classes work your entire body on a special stationary exercise bicycle with a weighted flywheel. Some spin classes are operated like boot camps, usually in larger fitness centers, and can be extremely intense. However, I'm going to add a little spunk to my workout and attend a Soul Cycle class. Soul Cycle is 45 minutes of high energy cardio and body toning as you listen to empowering affirmations. The workout is low impact and allows you to control your own pace and level of resistance, but infuses good music and mood lighting while you cycle. Soul Cycle classes are only offered in larger cities like LA and New York. Kelly Ripa, Nicole Richie and our former first lady Michelle Obama are a few of the many celebrities who've become advocates of Soul Cycle.

There are many other alternative fitness options for you to choose from. They range from fun and enjoyable to unusual and eccentric. The list of alternative workouts below combine dance and cardio to engage your entire body and keep the momentum going.

- Belly Dancing
- Surfboarding
- Barre Classes
- Twerk Classes
- Kick Boxing
- Burlesque
- Pilates
- Kangoo Jump
- Cross Fit
- Trampoline
- Pole Dancing
- Boot Camps

Depending on the fitness center in your area, you may also have the option for virtual workout routines. When I relocated for my new position, the fitness center at my apartment complex offered virtual workouts. There were no instructor led classes, and I simply found a workout that suited my needs. Then I participated with others on the screen.

In your quest to become Fit, Fabulous and Focused, avoid fads and quick fixes like the Shake Weight, Ab Rocket, toning shoes, and sauna suits. These gimmicks and gadgets don't offer true fitness solutions and will eventually end up in the corner of your garage, collecting dust and taking up space.

Quick tip: if you are nervous about trying a new workout, visit a session in progress and experience firsthand what it offers. See if the class motivates you and gets your adrenaline flowing. After all, viewing images on Google and video clips on You Tube just isn't the same as actually being there. Throw on some cute workout gear, invest in a good pair of sneakers and keep an open mind.

As Zig Zigler said, "You don't have to be great to start, but you have to start to be great!" Believe me, there is a workout just waiting for you.

Be Consistent

Finding time to work out consistently can be a real challenge, especially if you are currently balancing work, personal life and family in your daily routine. You have to work late, you're tired, the kids have activities, you don't feel well, it's too cold, or it's too hot...let's face it—it's far too easy to find reasons to put your fitness goals on the back burner. Once you make the first excuse it becomes tempting to skip a day or two—or even three. Before you know it, you've stopped working out altogether.

Guess what? *You have to be stronger than your excuses!* Being consistent with your workout may be challenging, but your overall health is far too important to totally skip out on fitness. Now that you have committed to becoming Fit, Fabulous and Focused, there is no acceptable reason to neglect yourself. You should exert the same effort and energy to working out consistently as you would to making your weekly hair and nail appointments.

There are many benefits to working out consistently. Exercising helps you to maintain a healthy weight and can reduce the risk of diabetes, high blood pressure and heart disease. If you've spent a large portion of your day sitting at work, adding a consistent workout to your daily routine will also help to improve blood circulation and reduce stress. So that begs the question, "If working out consistently is so beneficial, why is it so hard to do?" The answer to the question is that you must find a way to make it not so difficult. I have a few tips to help you do just that.

Tip#1: Stop listening. Yes, stop listening to everyone else's idea of the perfect workout. Maybe your current schedule doesn't permit a 45 minute workout, but that doesn't mean you shouldn't work out. Start from where you are. 15 or 20 minutes a day will improve your health over time. Just do it consistently and the results will happen!

Tip#2: Make working out a priority. Move your workout to a higher position on your To-Do list. Choose days and times each week to work out and add your workout schedule as a weekly or daily appointment on your cellphone calendar. Treat it with the same priority as your other appointments. Your fitness goals are only as important as you make them.

Tip#3: Make it interesting. If being consistent is difficult for you, try joining an exercise class that interests you. Participating in a fitness class can alleviate the stress of figuring out what to do each day. It may also fuel ideas for additional workouts on your own. Working out doesn't have to be boring. It just has to be consistent!

Tip#4: Make it a Routine. Not a morning person? Then add your workout to your evening commute from work. Don't go home first. Stop by the gym or go to the park to get a thirty minute workout on your way home. Work up a good sweat, burn a few calories and take your mind off of work. If you are an early bird, try working out within the first 15 minutes after waking up. Get rejuvenated and energized before tackling your day. Routines build consistency in your workout plan.

Tip#5: Find a buddy or start a Fitness with Friends Meet Up group. The goal is to partner with other people who have similar fitness goals. Not everyone in the group needs to be a beginner, but it helps to have one or two people who can relate to your fitness challenges. If there's only two of you, that's even better. You can hold each other accountable and minimize canceled workouts. You can also create healthy competition and take advantage of two-person exercises. More importantly, you'll have more options as you build consistency in your workout routine.

Be Realistic

As much as I hate to admit it, your age will also play a role in how your body shapes up during your workout. Over time, certain body parts (like your rear end and boobs) will seem to develop a mind of their own. Don't let that revelation deter you from achieving your workout goals—it's all a part of your journey to becoming Fit, Fabulous and

Focused. A reputable personal trainer can help you target specific areas and achieve realistic results no matter your age. This doesn't mean that at age forty-five you can't have the same perky, round derrière as a twenty five year old. It just means that realistically you will have to work twice as hard to get the same results.

Once you've found the workout you love, take it one step further by setting a few realistic expectations and goals. Sitting at home watching celebrity-endorsed fitness infomercials (while hoping to achieve the same results) is probably not going to help if you only work out twenty minutes a day. It's going to take a little more effort than that. In my first book, *Pocket Guide to Pole Dancing*, the first chapter is titled "Change What You Can and Screw the Rest." It was devoted entirely to encouraging women to be realistic about beauty and fitness goals. It emphasizes the importance of worrying less about the things beyond your control, like wide hips and broad shoulders, while focusing more on enhancing the things within your control, like exercising, eating healthy, and makeup tips.

Being realistic means starting slow and building momentum. In the beginning, choose three days a week to exercise. Decide if you want to incorporate weekends too. Follow up by choosing the time you wish to exercise each day. Is a morning trip to the gym before heading to work appealing? Is a 30-minute walk during your lunch break or a two-hour sweat fest in the evening after work appealing? Choose what works best for you.

As you work toward your fitness goals, treat them like building blocks. Break larger goals into smaller ones. This will increase your chances of achieving precisely what you desire. As time progresses and you build consistency in your day-to-day fitness regimen, you can add new exercises or increase the duration of your work out session.

If you fall off the wagon once or twice, don't stop. Life happens. Simply regroup and continue with your daily routine. If you find that your workout time gets interrupted frequently, then consider changing your time or maybe altering your days. Being realistic about your workout will help you adjust as needed, but be careful not to confuse procrastination with interruptions. There is a difference. Shifting your workouts to different times and days to avoid working out is unacceptable. You are smart enough to know the difference!

Track Your Progress

In this day and age, the ability to track the progress of your workouts is literally at your fingertips. No more wall-hung fitness charts and outdated pocket calendars. There are mobile apps and online apps such as My Fitness Pal, Lose It, and Human that track your caloric intake and daily movement. Couch to 5k, Pocket Yoga, and PEAR Personal Coach are apps designed to coach, monitor, motivate and track your progress in the same manner as a personal trainer, but without the hefty price tag. If you prefer not to download multiple apps on your smartphone or mobile device, try using an activity tracker such as Fitbit and the Apple Watch Series 1. These activity trackers are wearable devices that are loaded and updated constantly with a variety of apps to help you achieve your fitness goals.

Before we continue, I know that in the over-forty crowd the word "app" is often used but sometimes not fully understood. No worries, I've got you covered. To ensure that we are speaking the same lingo throughout this section, I will attempt to explain what app actually means without being super technical. The word app is short for application. It is a software application that has been modified for use on smartphones and mobile devices. Apps allow you to access specific tasks like shopping, banking or couponing from your smartphone or mobile device without ever visiting a company's actual website or buying expensive software licenses. Apps like Retail Me Not and Amazon simplify the online shopping process, and practically every major bank offers an online banking app to its customers. Most apps are very user friendly even if you are not tech-savvy. They can be used wherever and whenever at your convenience.

Now that we are on the same wave length, let's get back to tracking your progress. If you are really looking to make a statement by tracking your fitness transformation, there are also apps such Fit Stitch that allow you to post pictures throughout your fitness journey. You can upload your before and after pictures via Fit Stitch to social media sites to inspire others or build a following on your favorite social media site. Other apps like the Watch Me Change app can be used to create short time-lapse videos using the photos you take each day on your mobile device. The videos can be uploaded or kept as a personal journal of your fitness progress.

And if all of these tech-savvy ideas are a little too intimidating for you, stick with the basics. Track your progress the old fashioned way in a spiral notebook or three-ring binder.

Get Inspired

Inspiration leads to motivation! Supermodels Iman and Naomi Campbell are my inspiration. We are approximately the same height and weight, and I admire their beauty, their persona and their business savvy. Whenever I enter a room, speak at meeting, or go out for a night on the town, I envision myself working the runway like Naomi Campbell and turning heads like Iman. It's such a confidence booster and I've done it for years. I remember watching Naomi Campbell walk the runway of the Victoria Secrets fashion shows, thinking, *Wow, she is the epitome of confidence and her legs are absolutely gorgeous.* In recent years, she has shared her dietary secrets, which include refraining from bread, pasta, and foods that are high in carbs. She eats plenty of leafy vegetables and protein-rich foods like eggs, meat, fish and cheese. She also refrains from alcohol and smoking and detoxes her body at least three times a year. Her workout routine includes Pilates and yoga.

Now that I've added a few more pounds than usual to my 5' 10" frame, I'm inspired to incorporate a few of Naomi's diet and exercise tips into my daily routine. I also printed 8X10 color photos of Naomi and Iman and posted them on my vision board to inspire me during my workouts. There are other women who inspire me to achieve greatness in other areas, but as for my physical inspirations, Naomi and Iman are my faves.

The person who inspires you physically doesn't have to be a national celebrity. She could be someone in your neighborhood, your church, a coworker, or someone in your family. The inspiration to get in shape and workout consistently can come from multiple sources. So take some time to think about it and identify your muse. If possible, post pictures of them on your vision board or save their photos as your screen saver. Look at the photos often to remind yourself of your fitness goals. Adopt a few of that person's fitness habits as your own. When you find a source of inspiration, there's no need to reinvent the wheel...just realign it!

30-Day Workout Challenges

Imitation is the highest form of flattery, right? And if imitation can help you conquer new goals, then by all means identify your role model and follow her example!

The following 30-Day challenges for working out will propel you closer to what you personally envision.

30-Day Plank Challenge:

- The 30-day plank challenge only has one exercise which you have to do each day.
- Slowly build up your strength and core muscles by increasing the length of time each day.
- Gradually increase the time of your exercise until you reach a goal predetermined by you. (i.e. hold it for 60 seconds or 90 seconds).

30-Day Little Black Dress Challenge:

- Work on toning up a part of your body for thirty days. It can be your butt, abs, legs, arms, etc.
- After thirty days, put on your favorite little black dress and accentuate the body part you worked on during the thirty day period.

30-Day Hydrate your Body Challenge:

- Drink water and only water for thirty days. You may not get to eight glasses per day, but you must drink water for thirty days.
- No caffeine, no sodas, no coffee, or juices. Only water.
- Try to increase your water intake each day. You cannot drink less water than you did the previous day.

30-Day Get Outside Challenge:

- Take a break from the computer, the iPhone, the tablet and all of your other electronic gadgets.

- Every day, at least once a day, spend 20 minutes outside and take in some fresh air.
- Sit on the porch/deck.
- Walk the dog.
- Blow leaves or snow off the driveway.
- Water the flowers.
- Go for a walk.
- Ride a bike.

There you have it! These tips will have you waking up with anticipation, working out with determination, and going to bed with satisfaction!

CHAPTER 3

Learn to Say No

Learning to say "NO" didn't come easy for me. I had to figure it out through trial and error. That's because all I'd ever known was to insert my energy, my time, my resources, and my money into solving a problem. It's what my parents did. It's what I learned to do.

During my thirties, my solution to problem solving was to act first and think later. This method was always accompanied by a tidal wave of emotions and a whole lot of stress. I needed tools to be a strategic thinker, but lacked them. Back then my life events seemed to move twice as fast as the life events of my peers, and there weren't a lot of self-help books and Internet blogs to provide the insight I needed.

Whether it was a close family member with a problem, a distant relative from years ago, or a friend of a friend, my instinctive response was to fix it, make it better, take care of it, or handle it. Initially people began to rely upon me for help, and it felt great. But then they began to expect it. I found myself helping others even at the expense of my own livelihood and financial well-being. When I couldn't or didn't help, my "dependents" were "let down" and the criticism was overwhelming. I had unwittingly positioned myself as "the fixer," complete with a flock of needy followers who refused to give me a break. I felt like Atlas holding the world on my shoulders, and I slowly grew to resent it. But the guilt I felt for not getting involved was almost unbearable, not to mention my worry over "who else was going to take care of it?" That was the problem in a nutshell. I felt that I could not say "NO."

Finally, I started to think of ways to do just that—say "NO." Then I found myself waist deep in solicited and unsolicited advice. Associates, friends and colleagues shared stories and opinions about the best way to start the process and made it all sound so easy (and at times unbelievable). It was as if I was the only one in my circle who struggled with the notion of letting others down. I remember thinking, *What's wrong with me and why is this so difficult?*

I found myself on an emotional roller coaster as I wrestled with the concept. But deep down, I knew that learning to say "NO" would free up my resources and allow me the time I needed to create the life I wanted. I just had to find the courage, nerve, and the discipline to put the concept into practice.

One day, a few months before my fortieth birthday, I sat at my favorite hangout, Barnes & Noble. While sipping a hazelnut latte, I spotted a quote written on a coffee mug. It read, "Simplify your life. Say No." Even though I've read plenty of quotes about simplifying my life, I'd never seen it spelled out so succinctly. It was basic. It was profound. It was just what I needed. I felt like the last seven years had been an experiment in spinning my wheels, and then a simple quote on a mug became the exact tool I needed to stop the madness. Now I knew exactly what I needed to do. I had to say "NO" not only to relatives and friends, but also to my self-defeating behaviors.

Imagine that. My A-HA moment came when I realized that being able to say YES didn't obligate me to say YES. Saying NO was an option and had always been. It was just an option I choose not to previously exercise because of my own self-defeating behaviors. These lessons were like chicken soup for my stressed out soul. After relishing the moment a while longer, I finished my latte and began writing an action plan! I pledged the following:

- I will say NO to my instinctive ability to fix things for others.
- I will say NO to my dominant desire to lead and take charge.
- I will say NO to my fear of what will happen if I don't intervene.
- I will say NO to my small thinking and old way of problem solving.

I was now on my way to saying NO to my self-defeating behaviors and saying YES to creating the life I wanted after forty. #gameon

Tell Your Children "NO"

Saying NO to family is definitely easier said than done. This includes saying no to our kids and grandkids. As women, we thrive on the concept of being able to give them the things we didn't have while growing up. But sometimes we allow this concept to get way out of hand. Before we know it, our children have all the latest electronic gadgets, the most popular video games, and own more name brand clothing than a small clothing boutique. They may even drive a better car than we do. If left unchecked, this concept perpetuates even further and creates a false sense of entitlement.

As mothers, we often become obsessed with providing the perfect life for our kids. We cater to their requests no matter how unreasonable at times, not realizing that our behavior can be detrimental to their growth into adulthood. After all, the real world isn't perfect and they won't always get what they want. Kids need to develop skill sets that enable them to deal with that. Our inability to say NO along with our innate desire to fix things doesn't equip our children to solve their own problems. It doesn't motivate them to become totally self-sufficient. On the contrary, by saying YES, we spoil them and create a sense of instant gratification. We set them up for failure instead of building them into the young adults they are meant to be—Adults who know how to move mountains and make things happen for themselves and their families.

Now, I'm not advocating that you let your kids go without a few fun indulgences, negate their requests for assistance, or deprive them of occasional splurges. But if you find yourself saying yes to their every whim or solving every crisis in their lives, it's time to take a good hard look at your parenting style. Our job is to give them every thing they need and some of what they want, and that can only happen by setting boundaries for yourself and them. If you find it difficult, try the following tips:

- Set limits. Only allow yourself to say yes to things under a certain dollar amount. A small dollar amount!
- Encourage patience: Tell them they can have the item for their birthday or at Christmas or some other special occasion.
- Build problem solving skills: Allow your teenager or young adult to solve their own crisis using their own resources. If they don't have the resources, allow them to figure out how to obtain those resources and what to do next. Don't pitch in or fill in the gap.

You don't have to try all of these tips at once. Choose one and stick to it. Eventually saying NO will become your normal practice, and your kids will develop the initiative to either fund their own extravagances, or find the patience to wait for special occasions.

You'll inevitably experience feelings of guilt or the temptation to waiver once you make the decision to say NO, but you must stand firm. You must strive to avoid emotional confrontations with your children or other family members. Once you've communicated your answer and given an explanation (only if you feel the need to do so), move on. Don't lie. Don't embellish the truth or make up some gigantic fable that you have to remember years from now. You simply say NO. Once you do it the first couple of times, it gets easier.

Tip: Saying NO to family is the first step in redirecting your resources to create the life you want.

Tell Your Boss NO

Creating the life you want after forty means that you must respect and value your time so that others will too. If you find yourself complaining about the long hours or feeling undervalued at work, your boss may not always be the problem. Perhaps your inability to say "NO" to your boss is the problem.

Despite what your employer wants you to believe, there is such a thing as Work-Life Balance, which simply means that our personal lives are just as important (possibly even more important) than our professional lives. It's unbelievable the amount of hours we spend on our jobs in the name of "success." I realize there are several positions out there that may require fifty and sixty hour workweeks. You may be next in line for that long awaited promotion or partnership with the company. You could also absolutely LOVE your job or have a limited social life and welcome the long hours. There's nothing wrong with that. To those of you who feel this way, congratulations!

This conversation is for those women who are unhappy, unsatisfied and under-compensated in their current positions, but spend hours upon hours at the office hoping things will change. This is for those "salaried" divas who knowingly allow their boss to take advantage of their time and wreak havoc on their personal lives. You attend late meetings, come in early, take phone calls after work hours, work from home, skip lunch and stay late, only to find yourselves disappointed during your annual review because your raise does not reflect your dedication. If this is you, it's time to tell your boss "NO" and stop working for free.

Set boundaries on how late you are willing to work. Set limits on the amount of work you take home every day. Be proactive by scheduling a Saturday to avoid falling behind, or perhaps you can schedule late days at the office according to your availability and workload. Be clear and concise about the extra hours you can offer. If you are salaried and have scheduled commitments prior to the request for you to work late, make your boss aware of this. Do not allow him or her to monopolize your personal time, rearrange your priorities, or manipulate your daily routine with one unscheduled crisis after another.

If you are an hourly employee, make your boss aware of your weekday overtime availability or which Saturday of the month you can come in for a few hours. Of course, your boss may ask you to do "one more thing" after you've clocked out to go home. You may hear, "I need this first thing tomorrow morning!" as you walk out the door. These scenarios warrant overtime, not some ridiculous comp time arrangement. Do your homework by Googling your state and federal labor law websites for the latest information on overtime laws.

Tip: Saying NO to your boss allows you to value your time and utilize it to create the life you want.

Say "NO" to Your Partner/Spouse

Years ago I had a conversation with a dear friend who told me she was exhausted and needed to get some rest. She was a stay-at-home mom, and naturally I assumed that her kids were keeping her busy and causing her to stay awake at night. As we continued the conversation, she mentioned that she always had the kids fed, bathed and in bed according to their scheduled time of 8:30pm, yet she seemed so tired and drained. She was not attending college part time in the evenings and didn't mention a lot of outside activities other than the church choir. So I assumed it wasn't her social life that kept her up late. I finally stopped trying to figure it out for myself and I asked why she was so tired.

She explained that her husband liked his shirts freshly pressed for work, so she woke up at 5:00am every morning to tackle the ironing. At night, her husband also liked to watch the news and other late night television shows and preferred that they go to bed at the same time despite her schedule with the kids or how tired she may be. This ultra-devoted wife and mother managed to stay awake every night until her hubby turned off the television, and then got up at the crack of dawn to iron his shirts and take care of the children.

She also maintained all of her other duties by keeping a clean house, cooking dinner daily, grocery shopping, volunteering at school for the kids, choir rehearsal, entertaining friends and fulfilling her husband's intimate needs. The daily routine in addition to the late hours and early mornings was draining the life out of her. She constantly struggled to find better ways to manage her time and to avoid being tired, but it was to no avail.

Fast forward 20 years later to our fabulous forties. I asked this same friend if she had any advice for me, since I'm in a long-term relationship and new to the game. She immediately responded, "Learn to say NO to your partner. You won't go to hell for saying NO to your future husband. If he's the right one for you, he'll be willing to compromise." She is on her second marriage and no longer wakes up at 5:00am to iron shirts. In fact, my friend doesn't hesitate to tell her new husband NO, and they both are happier because of it. By the time we finished the conversation, I walked away with some sound advice and a few tips that are worth sharing.

- Set boundaries to create balance within your relationship.
- Find a compromise that works for both partners as much as possible
- Communicate your boundaries clearly so that your partner is aware.

Tip: Saying NO to your partner allows you to set boundaries and have balance as you create the life you want.

Say "NO" to Unproductive Habits

Are you a slave to "bad" habits like smoking, drinking, or over eating? Are you prone to "unproductive" habits that include procrastination, skipping meals, neglecting your health, excessive shopping, perfection, overcommitting, tardiness and aggressive driving? Just like a bad habit, getting rid of an unproductive habit takes the same level of commitment, practice, and continuous effort. Both bad habits and unproductive habits can be broken.

I read a very interesting article on Lifehack.org about breaking bad habits and was intrigued that the writer suggested we answer a few questions when saying "NO" to a bad habit:

- What will you do instead when you kick the unproductive habit?
- How will you spend the money you save from not spending it on the old habit?
- Do you really want to change?
- Is now the right time to break the habit?
- What's in it for you?

After reading the article, I felt inspired to purge the bad habits from my life, and this meant saying "NO." It required new levels of planning and discipline. It compelled me to also hone in on the hidden unproductive habits that lingered in my life.

The deceptive thing about an unproductive habit is that it may not have the visible, life-altering or self-destructive effects of a bad habit. Unproductive habits can go undetected for weeks, months, and even years before you acknowledge them. Yet they rob you of your most precious commodity—your time.

You can start the process of saying NO to unproductive habits with simple tweaks to your phone or mobile device. Remove easily accessed apps and you'll save time instead of wasting it! Clear the cache and the Internet search history on your laptop and computer to minimize the temptation of having easy access to your favorite sites. Download a free user-friendly budget app like Every Dollar by Dave Ramsey to monitor your spending and curtail your desire to overspend. Minimize the visual temptation to procrastinate or get back in bed for a few more minutes. Make your bed as soon as you wake up. Next, change the way you speak about unproductive habits. Instead of saying, "I can't do it today," or "Maybe some other time," try saying "I don't do that anymore," or "I gave that up." In other words, speak your new reality into existence.

Don't overwhelm yourself by trying to change your habits all at once. You'll end up frustrated and more stagnant than you were before. Instead, focus on changing one habit at a time. Concentrate on the benefits of saying "NO" to the unproductive habit and rejoice in the free time you will gain by getting those habits under control.

Tip: Saying NO to unproductive habits promotes self-discipline as you create the life you want.

Say "NO" to the Church

Being a part of the church community can be an important, satisfying and integral part of your life. Those who volunteer at church often say they are blessed to be a blessing to others. I totally agree. However, we can get so wrapped up in these spiritual extracurriculars that we become overextended.

Scratch the surface and you'll find dozens of ways to become involved...or over-involved. For instance, Vacation Bible School, Sunday school, children's church, youth choir, sick members ministry, new members ministry, singles, couples and widows ministries, outreach ministry, midday and evening bible study, choir rehearsal, praise team, music and dance ministry, leadership ministries, church conferences, Pastor's anniversary, church anniversary, mission trips and more can monopolize our time until we are depleted, rather than fulfilled.

You must say NO and set limits to the number of activities that you participate and volunteer in weekly, especially if you have children and/or a spouse who participates actively as well. The truth is, the good Lord does not require you to physically burn out, nor does He want you to neglect other important facets of life. Be mindful of over-extending yourself financially, as well. Additional church activities may require monetary commitments beyond the regular tithes and offerings. The decision to participate should not be made hastily or taken lightly.

So YES, it's okay to say NO to the church. Discuss the required commitment of your time and resources with your significant other before making a decision to volunteer. Ask specific questions and give yourself a day or two to respond. You benefit no one by making a hasty decision, only to experience resentment or remorse later.

Certainly being a Christian requires sacrifice, but God wants us to give with a happy heart—not a heart burdened with anxiety, stress and doubt.

Tip: Saying NO to the church encourages time-management as you create the life you want.

Say "NO" to Your Social Life

Are you the person who attends every social function, concert, wine tasting and mixer happening in your city? Is your social calendar consistently overbooked with events while your To Do list remains hopelessly incomplete? Are you plagued by FOMO—the "fear of missing out?" Being the life of the party and making an appearance at functions can be both exciting and exhausting, but as you create the life you want after forty, sometimes you have say "NO" to the fun and "YES" to your overall goals.

Until I began researching material to write this book, I had never heard of FOMO, the fear of missing out. The term, created by Millennials and added to the Oxford English Dictionary in 2013, describes an anxiety or emotion associated with the constant fear that you are missing out on the next big thing or an interesting event. The emotional effects of FOMO are real, and recent studies surrounding the impact of those effects have become more prevalent as the oversharing of life events and personal achievements have become the new norm on social media.

Certainly, staying connected and building relationships is essential to the soul. However, you shouldn't be required to attend every concert, road trip, spa day, and birthday celebration in order to maintain your social status. Step out of the spotlight to decompress, to focus on your goals, and to work on your game plan. If spending time alone is a difficult challenge, try making yourself less accessible by taking a temporary break from social media for thirty days. You'll begin to appreciate the lack of distraction.

So when your Bestie calls you for a girl's night out or your coworkers want to grab dinner after work or your clique presents the perfect impromptu weekend get-a-way, you have to say NO. Keeping an over-saturated social calendar can hinder your journey to becoming Fit, Fabulous and Focused. When you have important deadlines to meet and personal goals to accomplish, then social activities become wasteful distractions that can impede your progress.

Say NO to an excessive social life by establishing boundaries within your inner circle. Share your goals and priorities with your friends so they will understand your quest. Find creative work-arounds that allow you to mingle without undermining your goals. Consider a girl's night in and host a vision board party. Invite friends to work out with you. This will allow you to spend quality time with people who support your new Fit, Fabulous and Focused lifestyle.

Tip: Saying NO to your social life allows you to focus on your goals as you create the life you want.

Say "NO" to Drama and Negativity

In the era of Reality TV shows like the Real Housewives, Dance Moms, Mob Wives, Love and Hip Hop and other drama-filled shows, it's easy to become fascinated with the all of the hoopla. Watching grown adults argue, tell others off, set the record straight, and as they say on social media "clap back," is typically not as rewarding as the media portrays. It's actually quite unproductive.

Finding yourself at the center of drama and negativity after the age of forty is a clear indicator that it's time to reevaluate your choices and behaviors. What are you doing to repeatedly attract these outcomes? Are you being emotionally manipulated? Does your inability to say NO to drama land you in regrettable situations that could have been avoided? There are at least a dozen ways to identify how you invite drama and negativity in your life. My goal in this section is to give you guidance on how to say NO and put a stop to it.

It is not enough to simply switch off Reality TV shows or block someone on social media. You must reprogram your way of thinking and consciously work to modify the behaviors that lead you down this path in the first place. Drama and negativity doesn't just show up in your life every day—it's usually invited. Pay closer attention to the conversations you entertain and the content of those conversations. Be selective in who you allow into your inner circle.

Don't answer the call or text if there is negativity on the other end. Don't respond. Allow time to pass before you engage in a conversation or a situation that could escalate into drama. Know your limits and standards. You don't have to listen just because someone else feels like sharing.

Agree to disagree with the other party. Walk away or end the call on a positive note. Let go of the unhealthy relationships in your life that encourage negative behavior.

Leading a Fit, Fabulous and Focused life requires you to take responsibility for your actions and reactions. This may take lots of practice and discipline, especially if overreaction has become the norm. But it's much better to forsake the drama and negativity than have it consume your precious time.

Tip: Saying NO to drama and negativity develops positive thinking as you create the life you want.

Tell Your Creditors "NO"

Let me premise this section by saying that we should be good stewards of our money, and other people's money. We should pay back what we borrow. Others should pay back what we lend them. However, the reality is that situations can arise that are totally outside of our control. A job loss is one example. Illness is another. The same goes for divorce.

If you are in a financial bind and don't have the money to satisfy all of your creditors, it is okay tell them NO. You have the right to do so. Tell them NO and offer a reasonable plan in writing to pay them on new terms that fit your current situation. You do not have to accept payment arrangements that cause you further financial distress. Even if your current situation is a temporary one, you can still tell your creditors NO and make a new plan. But you have to be firm, communicate your plan, and stick to it.

Most financial planners will advise you to set aside six times your monthly income in a savings account to offset emergencies, but we all know that life doesn't always work that way. Working in the financial arena, I've witnessed many women who have lost income for any number of reasons, but they failed to renegotiate with their creditors. They either procrastinated because the situation felt uncomfortable or embarrassing, or they were just completely paralyzed with fear. Managing their finances seemed impossible, so they opened themselves to drastic repercussions such as garnishments, foreclosures and repossessions.

Learning to say NO to your creditors allows you to create financial solutions that work for your financial situation until you are able to pay more. No matter how aggressive and intimidating your creditors may sound on the phone or how often they send letters, you have the option to say NO and provide a counter offer. Remember, YOU are ultimately responsible for repaying your debts according to the terms YOU agree upon.

Do not make unrealistic payment arrangements that cause you to lose sleep or make you feel stressed throughout the day. Your creditors would much rather collect your money than to repossess the item you purchased several months or even years ago. Make affordable arrangements and write them down on your calendar as a reminder. Make every effort to successfully complete the new arrangement. Being Fit, Fabulous and Focused is about taking charge of your finances. The first step in doing so is learning when to say NO to your creditors.

Be inspired by a quote by J.K. Rowling: "Rock bottom became the solid foundation on which I built my life."

Tip: Saying NO to your creditors allows you take control of your finances as you create the life you want. Chapter 8 addresses the topic of fiscal fitness in much further depth, so keep forging ahead!

30-Day Challenges – Learn to Say "NO"

Whether it's family, church, friends, or self-defeating behaviors, learning to say NO is essential to building healthy relationships, establishing boundaries and creating a solid foundation for the life you want after forty. But learning to say NO doesn't happen overnight. You have to retrain your brain. Try your hand at a few of these 30-day challenges to kick-start your quest to say NO.

Quit a Bad Habit for 30 Days (to yourself):

- Give up games on your smart phone, eating fast food everyday, nail biting, smoking cigarettes, recreational drugs, eating sweets everyday, drinking alcohol excessively, or too much caffeine.
- Challenge yourself to kick at least one of those bad habits for thirty days.

No Apologies 30-day Challenge:

- Don't feel guilty after saying NO. Don't change your mind and cave in later.
- Don't apologize or offer excuses for saying NO.
- Do not be deceitful or lie.

30-Day Set Boundaries and Limitations Challenge (to others):

- For the next thirty days, whenever you say NO but feel guilty, write down all of the things you are saying YES to.
- Spend more quality time with family and friends.
- Take time to do things you like (i.e. hobbies).
- Enjoy having a reasonable and manageable workload.
- Appreciate the relaxation and peace of mind.

Before you know it, you'll embrace the positive and forsake the negatives. Your outlook will be brighter because you've banished the negative factors from your personal and professional life.

CHAPTER 4

Manage Your Emotions

Let's face it, ladies. We can be quite emotional. By the age of forty, hormonal fluctuations affect every part of lives. We endure cramps, bloating, mood swings, sore breasts, PMS, late pregnancies, hot flashes, perimenopause and full blown menopause. We stress over our weight, our appearance, our food intake, and our relationships with others. But apart from our hormones, we may have experienced post-traumatic stress from past events and not even realize it. We may struggle with unresolved issues that, quite frankly, require therapy. It's no wonder that we morph into emotional creatures from time to time (some of us more so than others).

YES! We are emotional. But being slaves to emotional triggers isn't something any of us should aspire to, regardless of the hormonal cauldron bubbling within our bodies. We can't allow our feelings to spiral out of control despite deep-seated or unresolved issues. We don't get a "emotional pass" for bad behavior, and we don't get excused for our constant discontentment.

For instance, we may hold grudges for an eternity, host pity parties at a moment's notice, and throw a bitchfest at the most inopportune place and time. But "losing it" does not paint a pretty picture, nor is it a strategic move. It is counter-productive in our journey to be Fit, Fabulous and Focused! The key to being successful in our varied emotional states is managing those emotions to ensure the best possible outcome.

Now before we move further along in this chapter, let the record show that I am not suggesting we suppress our emotions or deny our feelings. That could be both mentally and physically unhealthy. I am asking, however, that you manage your emotional "reactions" so that you can remain in control and make moves that benefit YOU. There is a distinct difference. For some of us, it's not easy being cerebral and tactical in our responses, especially when a moody urge threatens to overpower our better judgement. I know from my own personal experiences that managing these reactions is easier said than done. The good news is that it CAN be done.

Here's an example of a situation in which I set several heads of hair on fire—not literally, but certainly figuratively. I was wrapping up my very last day at my previous job and had reached the maximum point of frustration during a conversation with my almost-former boss. I was totally fed up with his manipulative tactics and condescending remarks. As a result of not managing my emotions well, I emailed him a scathing letter expressing my thoughts about his overall behavior and character. I called him a "hater" and asked him to kiss my entire ass at the end of the email. I proofread it for errors and wasted no time clicking the send button.

Typically when I write an emotional email correspondence to someone, I utilize my personal forty-eight hour protocol, which is first to write the email, then save it as a draft copy. I re-read the email after waiting forty-eight hours and finally, if I feel the same way after this "cooling off" period, I send it to the intended recipient. If I do not feel the same, I delete the email and forgo the response altogether, or write a new email with less emotion. I have used this practice for several years, and it works wonderfully!

However, in this scenario with my former director, I ignored my own forty-eight hour protocol and allowed my emotions to get the best of me. I even copied his directors on the email! I wanted to be done with him and did not want to take the baggage with me on my new endeavor. So I purged my emotions at the keyboard, feeling vindicated and victorious. I had set the record straight in no uncertain terms.

Then I shared the email with a couple of my closest coworkers for grins and giggles before logging off my computer one final time. Of course from my co-workers point of view, the letter was indeed a riveting topic for office gossip. In fact, it trended for several days after my departure from the organization. I was told the letter bore a slight resemblance to a Julia Sugarbaker rant from my favorite show back in the '90s, "Designing Women". But on a professional level, I clearly did not do a great job of managing my reaction to my emotions. I went "nuclear" in a situation where a bit more tact would have produced the same results...all because I was triggered.

It took a few days of soul searching, but I eventually admitted to myself that I could have chosen a different, less abrasive way to convey my frustration and end my relationship with my director. I used that encounter as a pivotal moment in my career and decided to work on managing my emotions in future scenarios. My first challenge was to identify my emotional triggers.

Know Your Emotional Triggers

A trigger is a response to a person, event, dialogue, or other situation that provokes a strong emotional reaction. We may not necessarily be aware of our triggers, even though we may have several. Different people, places and things can trigger a childhood trauma or resurrect a painful moment that still percolates under the surface. When we are haunted by the past, the past still has the power to trigger our emotions in the blink of an eye. But recent events can also trigger us. Injustice, disrespect and slights can trigger us.

For some, any unpleasant matter involving our children or significant others can provoke an immediate emotional outburst. Our instinct to defend and protect can turn us into scary and formidable beasts. Sometimes wounded pride is a trigger that "unleashes the Kracken." We may be triggered by primal fears, lack of safety, jealousy, criticism, guilt, love, shame, betrayal, embarrassment, rejection, etc. Your feelings may boil over once you have reach the pinnacle of disgust. It all depends on what is deeply important to you, and why. This is why a situation may trigger other women, but not trigger you at all, and vice versa.

As you continue your journey to create the life you want after forty, an important task is learning to manage your reactions to your emotions. It is critical in your personal and professional development. Despite how you may feel, you can't go around slaying dragons or withdrawing from others or having an emotional meltdown every time you are tested. There may be days ahead when your teenage son or young adult daughter trigger your emotions by defying the perfect plan you've laid out for their lives. I'm sure there will come a time when your coworker or even your boss will work your last nerve as you struggle to maintain your composure in their presence. There are also those moments when your significant other will test your boundaries, your patience and your resilience throughout your day-to-day interactions.

Be not dismayed! You can survive all of these emotional occurrences and still maintain your poise, dignity and a moderate blood pressure reading. But this only happens if you exercise diligence and identify your emotional triggers as they happen. Get to know yourself. Be honest. By doing so, you will become more aware of the feelings associated with your triggers and gain the power to respond differently. Eventually you will be in control, rather than being controlled. This will produce a more desirable—and classy—outcome.

Keep a Journal

Start monitoring the moments that take you on an emotional roller coaster. Write them down in your journal as they happen. Then ask yourself, *What triggered that moment?* What were you feeling? What were you thinking? Repeat this process as often as needed. Keeping a journal will help you identify your common triggers and the deeper root causes. It will also allow you to recognize your triggers as they happen, which in turn will help you respond appropriately.

Heal Your Spirit

Life has lots of teachable moments. Forgive yourself for those emotionally triggered melt-downs and vow to learn from them. Then take care of yourself. Pamper your body and love yourself. The process of healing may include both physical and mental reconditioning. Visit a spa, take long baths, go for a walk, go to a comedy show, indulge in pedicures, manicures, facials, massages, take a yoga class, take a dance class and seek counseling if needed.

Make it a Priority

The responsibility of managing your emotions is one of your highest priorities! This step is essential to your personal evolution and can bolster your efforts to create the life you want after forty! Managing your emotional reactions is a necessary building block for further growth. Chapter Five (Upgrading Your Perspective) gives additional pointers, so hang on! More help is coming your way, I promise!

Don't take it Personally

We function in a digital society and rely heavily upon electronic communication. With limited or no personal interaction to clarify meaning, our instant messaging, email, texting and tweets can backfire and offend without us even realizing it. Things get lost or misconstrued in translation.

For example, using all caps in an email, ignoring an instant message when your status shows that you are online, group texting without consent, and even using the wrong emoji can all be considered offensive in the online world. When posting your comments on social media and expressing your opinion via the relatively new phenomenon of hash-tags, it's easy for others to take things out of context, and vice versa. People may assume the worst, even when an "insult" is unintentional.

Additionally, there are still "old fashioned" ways to offend others, such as walking past someone or entering a room without saying hello, or not answering a phone call from a loved one as expected. The list goes on and on. If you are on the giving or receiving end and find yourself becoming annoyed, then it's time to grow some thicker skin and stop sweating the small stuff. Before you make assumptions or determine someone else's intent, use the following tips to avoid taking their actions personally.

- Put yourself in someone else's shoes.
- Stop giving power to someone else's words.
- Don't jump to conclusions. Ask for clarity.
- Let go of old baggage.
- Realize that it's not always about you.
- Resist the urge to be a keyboard warrior.

The Power of Choice

Have you ever been tempted to make a phone call out of anger? Have you felt the urge to get in your car and drive recklessly to your destination? Have you slammed a door, flipped the bird, or cut an annoying driver off as he or she tried to change lanes? Have you, like me, clicked the send button on that email to end a business relationship gone wrong?

Then it's time to press pause and take a moment to think! Consider the consequences that may occur because of your next impulsive decision. Don't make hasty moves that can result in permanent or life-altering disasters. Be aware when you are feeling emotional. This is a key component in managing your reactions. Give yourself time to calm down and process your feelings before making a move. Whenever possible, play the conversation or situation in your mind before it happens. Anticipate possible outcomes and your responses to each of those outcomes. Get ahead of your emotional triggers by identifying what could set you off and plan for a favorable result. There is no guarantee that things will happen exactly as you imagine, but at least you will be prepared.

Thinking before taking action is not always about avoiding conflict. Losing control can be a reflection of insecurities, an indication of low self-esteem, or a symptom of self-defeating behaviors (SDBs). SDBs, especially, cause us to make costly emotional decisions against our better judgment. Decisions such as accepting a marriage proposal from Mr. Wrong, moving in with an incompatible mate, or cosigning for the financial obligations of family members are all examples of SDBs. Likewise, hiring a friend who is not qualified for a position is a sign that SDBs are in play. Buying luxury items to keep up with your colleagues is simply masking your feelings of inferiority within your social circle. The scenarios discussed above are driven by feelings of guilt, fear, loneliness, obligation, false pride, peer pressure, and misplaced loyalty, which are merely the tip of the iceberg when it comes to self-defeating behaviors.

Be completely honest with yourself and analyze your own SDBs. You will take giant steps toward defeating the cycle of poor decisions by "owning" your flaws and fixing them. Make choices that benefit you. Period.

Pity Parties

It seems only natural to call your Bestie or invite a few girlfriends over to help you get over an emotional mishap. It may be tempting to call up the ex-boyfriend to comfort you through the night. You might even call in sick the next day at work or leave early because you are feeling blue. But these scenarios are only temporary solutions to emotional states and solve nothing in the long run. Avoid the temptation to ask others to validate your impulsivity. The last thing you need is for someone else to prop you up when you are behaving irrationally. After all, feeling sorry for yourself is one thing, but inviting others to join in is a surefire way to perpetuate the negative momentum. It's time to stop making the same emotional mistakes again and again.

So the next time you're feeling sorry for yourself, don't call upon others to endorse your emotions. Make sure your support group includes people who will listen objectively and be honest with you. Our best resources are those who are sensible enough to help us avoid mistakes. And you can rely on yourself, as well. Spend time alone, write in your journal, or have a good cry. Do what it takes to get it out of your system and then move on!

Being the Victim

You're forty now. It's time to accept that everything happening to you is not someone else's fault. The choices you make and have made are your own responsibility. As long as you continue to blame others for your status in life or the dreams you did not pursue, you will remain stuck in the past. You must learn to forgive and let go of bitterness and anger, especially if these negative emotions prevent you from pursuing your own dreams.

You may never get an apology from your spouse. A loved one who hurt you may never ask for forgiveness. You may not get affirmation from your parents, or gratitude from those you have helped. It is imperative that you accept it and get beyond it. YOU are responsible for your own happiness. Acknowledge your role in the experience and move on.

Remember, change begins with you.

Boost Your Self Confidence

Managing your emotions will be less daunting if you focus intently on improving your self-esteem and self-confidence. You'll worry less about what others think and learn to love yourself more when you stop showing up at your own pity parties. If you are on a budget, don't stress about perfecting your image. There are plenty of inexpensive ideas and tips you can incorporate to boost your self-confidence and self-esteem without breaking the bank.

For my birthday, I decided to get a makeover at a local MAC Cosmetics counter. The makeup artist recommended faux lashes instead of mascara. I'd worn them a few times on special occasions, but hadn't given them a second thought in years. So I figured why not, it's a special occasion…it's my birthday! After celebrating my birthday in faux lashes, I decided to wear them for the rest of the week. The response was unbelievable! The next day at work I received tons of compliments about my "new look." It was almost as if I had not worked with those same people the day before. So that small purchase of faux lashes became a total boost to my self-confidence.

I know there's already enough media propaganda focusing on your looks and body image, and this conversation isn't about convincing you to look like someone else. But it is about accentuating who you already are—a beautiful person, both inside and out. So go ahead and try one or all of the confidence building tips below to boost your self-esteem:

- Focus on being healthy at your current weight.
- Enhance your natural beauty. Try wearing less makeup and focus on skin care.
- Change your lipstick color or try faux lashes to enhance your eyes.
- Accentuate your outfit with a silk scarf or new accessories.
- Try a new hair color or haircut as the seasons change.
- Buy a pair of skinny leg jeans or jeggings to flaunt your curves.
- Dress up twice a week, even if work is business casual and jeans on Friday.
- Wear sexy lingerie to bed during the week even if you live alone.
- Get a manicure or try a lightly scented hand lotion.
- Exercise outdoors once a week to enjoy the sun and the scenery.
- Add a few splashes of a scented body spray before going out on the town.
- When dining alone, dress to impress and dine at a popular restaurant. Enjoy the compliments and attention you receive as the evening progresses.

30-Day Emotional Challenges

Are you ready to be challenged? From time to time we all get a little emotional, so experiment with one (or all) of the challenges below to help curtail your emotional lows. It will help you better understand yourself and your triggers.

Manage Your Emotions for 30 Days:

- Don't raise your voice to get your point across.
- Don't yell or argue during conversations. Communicate in a normal tone with your kids, spouse, coworkers, colleagues, friends, etc.
- Maintain your composure. Find less aggressive ways to communicate to others.

No Complaining for 30 Days:

- Challenge yourself to be complaint free.
- No complaining about your job, your mate, your children, or your social life.
- No complaining about someone else's job, mate, children, or social life.

Keep a Gratitude Journal for 30 Days:

- Write something every day in your journal about why you are grateful.
- Do a little soul searching, count your blessings each day, and journalize your thoughts.

Potty Mouth Challenge (No Cursing for 30 Days):

- Stop swearing.
- Set a monetary amount to put in a jar each time you swear. It needs to be at least fifty cents per word.
- At the end of the month, donate the proceeds to someone in need or to a charitable cause.
- Stop and do 25 sit-ups or 15 push-ups each time you swear.

Do you feel more empowered now that you have taken responsibility for your emotional state? You should! By making a commitment to being classy and in control, you'll attract more positivity and less drama into your life.

Fabulous
(The Power of Choice)

Now that you have read the first four chapters in this book and completed the accompanying 30-day challenges in your Fit, Fabulous and Focused workbook, you are ready to pursue a fabulous life. Being fabulous in this self-help guide isn't about glamour, glitz and luxury living as the media would have us all to believe.

It's about:

- *Taking charge of your destiny and defining your own happiness.*
- *Living life on your own terms, even if those terms are different than everyone else's.*
- *Embracing change and understanding the power of choice.*
- *Evolving into the person you were meant to be.*

The following chapters will require a little bit of soul searching to achieve this next level. I will be asking you to peel back a few layers and get to know yourself better. That means challenging and perhaps changing some of the beliefs you hold near and dear. During my own journey to become Fit, Fabulous and Focused, I encountered several moments that challenged me to my very core and redefined my outlook on life. For example, starting a new career as a single parent, watching my mother's painful battle with colon cancer, and becoming a grandmother multiple times in my thirties were all defining moments. At times, those moments were extremely difficult and indescribably unbearable. Yet, those same moments yielded some of the most valuable and rewarding lessons of my life. Those same moments propelled me to "choose" to live a fabulous life.

I also realized that living fabulously doesn't happen when you acquire glitz, glamour, or luxury—that's the superficial part of living fabulously. The authentic part of a fabulous life occurs when you embrace change and exercise the power of choice in your everyday life. Perhaps you wish to reinvent yourself and pursue a different path, or change your perspective after twenty years of thinking the same way. Upon completing this section of the book and the thirty day challenges, you will understand that living a fabulous life is not a matter of entitlement, it's a matter of choice.

I choose to live a fabulous life! You can too!

CHAPTER 5

Upgrade Your Perspective

Three months after the grand opening of my studio, business wasn't exactly pouring in the way I envisioned. It wasn't that the community wasn't interested in pole fitness…on the contrary! My phone rang constantly with inquiries about my classes and my website hits were increasing daily. But those inquiries were not converting into class enrollment or generating revenue. I became very frustrated and began to question my ability to make my business work.

One evening as I arrived at the studio a little early, I stopped by to visit Tony, one of the neighboring business owners. He owned the barbershop in the same business complex and had become like a mentor to me as I navigated the waters as a new entrepreneur.

He asked me if I was aware that potential customers were stopping by on the days when my studio was not open. I told him, "No." He also asked if my business hours were posted on my door. I replied, "No." I explained my strategy was to keep my overhead low by only opening on the days that I had guaranteed parties or classes booked in advance. I was a new business and wanted to cut costs in any way that I could. I figured the utility bills would be cheaper that way.

Tony paused for a moment and commented, "You know, I've been running my own barbershop for several years and can tell you that your business strategy is not going to work."

His comment was a little bold and I didn't really know how to handle the feedback. My first instinct was to get defensive and tune out what he had to say. But I hoped he had my best interest in mind, so I kept a level head and prepared myself for a good dose of constructive criticism.

Tony went on to explain that we were both in the service industry and that customers expected convenience as a part of great service. He said, "You are a new business, so if people continue to stop by and you are constantly unavailable, they will lose interest regardless of the service you offer." This certainly gave me a lot to think about, although at first I was hesitant about seeing things from his perspective. Even after accepting the wisdom of Tony's business advice, I was scared. After all, I was so strapped for cash at the time that every penny mattered.

But I decided to do exactly as he said. Tony had been a successful entrepreneur for years and it made sense to listen to someone who was where I wanted to be. So I maintained consistent and convenient hours for my customers and showed up every day at the same time—no excuses. It didn't matter whether I had customers booked or not, I was open for business. And just as Tony said, my customers found me and responded. I experienced an immediate increase in business over the next three months, from one class per week to two classes per day. My party bookings sky rocketed too.

Had I known the volume of customers who stopped by when I wasn't there, I would have stayed open all the time from the very beginning! After that teachable moment, I understood the importance and the value of seeing things from a different perspective. As you run your own business, you don't have to know everything, but you certainly have to be open-minded and willing to upgrade your perspective.

Old Habits Die Hard

What is a habit? Habits are behaviors that we repeat regularly, so that they become automatic. We form them in three interconnected ways: 1.) a cue, 2.) the behavior itself, and 3.) the reward. Through a bit of soul-searching, we can pinpoint some of the cues—or triggers—that cause us to respond subconsciously. This could be something as simple as seeing a wrinkle (the cue), and religiously applying a special cream (the behavior). We do this morning and night as part of our routine, and it becomes a habit that hopefully improves our complexion (the reward).

This is all fine and dandy, until we develop a habit that harms us. Spur-of-the-moment shopping sprees, cigarettes, checking email multiple times a day, overeating, excessive snacking, loaning money to friends, and maintaining unhealthy relationships are a few examples of negative habits that we may not even recognize as such. Our old habits reflect a fixed way of thinking—fixed, as in "inflexible" and "not easily changed." These ingrained behaviors may be stubborn. They may be hard to break. At some point you'll need to shed old habits and develop new ones. With time, practice, patience, and honesty, bad habits can be overcome. It's all a part of upgrading your perspective.

You can expect to feel emotional and overwhelmed when tackling negative habits. You'll have to part ways with the activities, people, and "comfort" you once frequently enjoyed. But you are in control. Once you realize that habits are associated with pleasure, impulse, or stress, you can wrestle those demons—and win. There's no one-size fits all formula to cure an old habit, and the length of time and effort it takes to break free varies from person to person. However, the process of shedding old habits is critical to reinventing yourself, or at least improving your health and wellness.

Keep in mind, new habits don't form overnight and old habits won't disappear in an instant. Overcoming an old habit is a process that requires a lot of focus. There will be days when it feels like you've finally overcome an old habit, only to find yourself frustrated and falling off the wagon again. I hear you! I have my own ongoing Facebook habit and must constantly remind myself that virtual reality isn't the same as living, breathing and growing offline. Sure, I like visiting Facebook to see what's going on in my social circle, especially since I don't see my family and friends as often as I'd like. But in my honest, self-assessing moments, I have to admit that the time spent on Facebook is counterproductive.

In fact, I would never have managed to finish this book if I constantly malingered on social media. Refraining, at least for me, was not as easy as it sounds because I was working with a mouse...and social media nirvana was just a mouse-click away! So I decided that whenever I was writing, I would refrain from using Facebook. At first my resolve lasted for several hours, and sometimes it lasted for only thirty minutes. It depended on how distracted I was before I started writing. To help me overcome this habit, I scheduled my writing sessions as appointments in my Outlook calendar at the same time every day, and I stuck to it. It caused me to form a new habit—writing—and became a true lesson in self-control and positive behavior. Now, thankfully, I only use social media during my downtime.

As you can see, once you make the decision to overcome an old habit, quitting cold turkey doesn't have to be the only solution. Like me, you may find it easier to replace the old habit with a new behavior. Try new things like walking after work, setting a monthly budget, tracking your spending, taking a Zumba class, living a smoke-free life or learning to swim. As you focus on the new behaviors, they will take precedence in your life and occupy your mind. Eventually you'll gravitate toward these new behaviors, and before you know it they'll become new, positive habits. Don't get frustrated if you temporarily falter. That's part of the process. Just start again where you left off and keep developing the new behavior.

Tip: "Lifestyle" change—or behavior change—can set you on a Fit, Fabulous and Focused path.

Change your Self-Talk

Another way to upgrade your perspective is to change the way you "talk" to yourself. Often we "talk" to ourselves based on the way we see ourselves. Imagine for a moment that you were the recipient of an award and were required to propose your own toast. What would you say about yourself? Or what if you were approached by the CEO of your company and asked to give a two-minute synopsis of why you should be promoted and receive a $20,000 bonus today. How would you respond?

I can honestly tell you that many of the women I know would not get the promotion or the bonus, because they would give themselves a less than worthy toast. Why? Because we often undervalue our strengths and present our talents in a less than convincing manner. If we appear emotional rather than confident, it's as if we don't believe in our own worth. Our "self-talk" damages our chances for growth. We become our own worst enemy without even realizing it.

Changing your "self-talk" starts from within. This means changing what you "think" about yourself, as well as what you tell yourself on a daily basis. It also means taming that doubtful inner voice and those negative thoughts that subconsciously surface whether you want them to or not. Refining your self-talk requires practice... sometimes lots of practice.

Maybe you've seen an episode of "Being Mary Jane" and noticed the positive affirmation Post It notes on her bathroom mirror. Perhaps you've seen the You Tube ads for Lunchbox Love with the positive affirmations for kids to read as they open their lunch boxes at school. Those moments are not just for television! They are simple and effective ways to change your "self-talk" and ultimately change your perspective. It's the conscious act of filling your mind with positive affirmations and reinforcements in the morning, at night and throughout the day.

Once I made the decision to change my "self-talk," I wrote six Post It notes and stuck them to my bathroom mirror. I now read them daily and add to them as needed. My Post It notes also include goals that I plan to achieve in the near future. You see, I knew that I had to change my "self-talk" if I wanted to upgrade my perspective.

Exercise #1: Change Your Self-Talk

Write three things you're currently doing. Write three things you want to achieve. Write three things you've already accomplished. See the examples below:

Currently: I graduated from a trade school.
Want to Achieve: I want to graduate from a university.

Accomplished: I talked to a college advisor and enrolled in classes.

_____

_____

_____

_____

Currently: I smoke cigarettes.
Want to Achieve: I want to quit smoking.
Accomplished: I talked to my doctor about a smoking cessation program and now have the tools to live free of tobacco.

_____

_____

_____

_____

Currently: I'm overweight.
Want to Achieve: I want to lose weight and get in shape.
Accomplished: I researched interesting exercise programs and can now pursue my health goals.

_____

_____

_____

_____

Change the Way You See Others

Changing the way you see others may challenge you to your very core. It takes major effort to step outside of the preconceived notions we've developed over the years. You may have to change your belief system and your behavior towards others—not an easy task. Belief systems and resulting behaviors are deeply rooted, and redefining them requires much more than simply changing an opinion or compromising with someone.

Your current beliefs may be strongly attached to religion, tradition, customs, culture and habits. While it is good to have values, it's just as good to recognize the prejudices and condescension we hold in our hearts. We should be willing to reevaluate our judgmental thoughts, words and deeds. Honest self-assessment can be emotionally challenging and exhausting, and this is probably the most difficult aspect of upgrading your perspective. But it is also one of the most essential components of the process. It all depends on how open minded and committed you are to growing as a human being.

For instance, we tend to form hasty generalizations and use other fallacies as a crutch. After all, lumping "types" of people into narrow categories is easier than actually getting to know someone personally. The truth is, reality is so much broader than the stereotypes we've invented. Our world isn't black or white...it contains lots of color, as well as shades of grey.

Getting started may be a little uncomfortable for you, but your desire to change is a strong indicator that you are ready. You can quietly change over time by taking small steps each day. For instance, attend a different church periodically, shop on a different side of town, eat lunch with different coworkers, volunteer to help others, or go on a date with someone of a different ethnicity. Make small incremental efforts to step out of your comfort zone and challenge your stagnant mindset. Participate in activities that will broaden your outlook and expose you to a different point of view. Take a closer, non-judgmental look at a specific person, place or a particular group of people.

Reconsidering the way we see others doesn't have to be an epiphany or huge a-ha moment. It doesn't have to be announced on social media posts or in motivational tweets. It can be as simple as surrounding yourself with people who support new beliefs and ideas. Perhaps get a mentor, a role model, or a life coach to help you change your mindset and behaviors. Don't wait! The sooner you get started, the better.

Live in the Present Moment

Have you ever heard the statement, "Live in the present moment?" I remember hearing the phrase years ago on the Oprah Winfrey Show. She made repeated references to living your best life and being present in the moment. But I never really understood what those phrases meant until I turned forty.

Although I'd accomplished several goals, worked full-time, and managed my dance studio, life became such a blur. There were many days that I couldn't account for, yet I know they happened. I had no real recollection of what each hour consisted of from one day to the next. Wake up, work, eat, sleep, and repeat. Wake up, work, eat, sleep, and repeat. I was on auto-pilot and wasn't fulfilled. Worse, life was literally passing me by one beautiful moment at a time. I was just too busy with day-to-day tasks and too focused on the future to actually enjoy the present.

At the time I was surrounded by others who were in the same boat. None of us were really living in the present moment. Instead, we were all just allowing life to happen. This is not an uncommon phenomenon among women, and it's usually not something we intend to do. Unforeseen circumstances and unexpected hiccups can cause us to close our eyes and "just get by." Add a few heartaches, and voila! We are no longer living in the present moment, but instead are living in the future or the past... anywhere but in the present.

If only women knew better, they would choose to participate in life wholeheartedly, right? So as you continue your journey to becoming Fit, Fabulous and Focused, you will no longer have to "go through the motions" and exist in a fog. Just as I did in my journey, you will have to make a conscious decision to upgrade your perspective by focusing on what matters to you right now. You will have to choose daily what is most important and become more aware of how you spend your time and focus your energy. You must become selective about the people, places and things you allow in your life. You must learn to block out or remove hindrances that keep you from living in the moment.

It will take effort to live in the present, because the same old distractions will reincarnate in one form or another for the rest of our lives. The change happens when you decide to relish the "here" and "now," rather than fretting about what happened or what's yet to be.

Make a list of all the upcoming activities you have planned and the groups and organizations in which you are an active participant, as well as the goals you are currently pursuing. As you review your list, ask yourself, "What excites me on this list? What am I passionate about more than anything else right now?" Once you have identified what brings you the most joy, you can make those items a priority above all else and learn to delegate or eliminate distractions that keep you from focusing on your goal. Now that you've gotten started, follow these tips to keep you focused on the present moment:

- Live life with a purpose.
- Take small steps towards your goal every day versus waiting for a special moment to make a huge change.
- Spend at least one hour each week making a list of all the things that you are grateful for in your life.
- Speak of your accomplishments without adding timelines such as years and dates. It makes your conversations more relevant.
- Use action verbs in your everyday conversation.

Celebrate Your Success

On the road to upgrading your perspective, you must learn to accept your blessings unapologetically and celebrate your gifts and talents—without explanation. You owe no one an explanation as you achieve your goals, accumulate wealth, or garner recognition for your success. Enjoy It! You worked hard to get to where you are in life. As you experience new successes, savor those moments. You earned it. Don't let the intrusive jealousy, nosiness and criticism of others dictate how you choose to enjoy your journey.

In fact, celebrating your success can be as elaborate or as private as you want it to be. The choice is yours to make, and yours alone. If you want to throw yourself a party, do it. Reward yourself with a trip. Do it! Upgrade your vehicle or give money to charity. Do it! Or you can keep it confidential if you like and simply accept that you are awesome. As I finished writing each chapter of this book, I took a moment to celebrate that "win" with a glass of wine. As you obtain your business license and Federal tax ID number to open your new business, share your accomplishment with your partner over a nice dinner. As you visit your Human Resources office to finalize your early retirement paperwork, pause to show gratitude and give thanks to God. The choice is yours.

Critics will always be there to tell you there is a more politically correct, more courteous, more inclusive, less arrogant way to recognize and celebrate your success. I say ignore them. Find your own special way to celebrate your milestones and progress along the way to becoming Fit, Fabulous and Focused.

Show Gratitude

As you evolve and upgrade your perspective in your daily life after forty, showing gratitude may already be part of your daily regimen. If not, it should. It costs you nothing to say "thank you" to a loved one, to show appreciation for a kind gesture, or to compliment a colleague. Gratitude can be shown with a handwritten note, a surprise visit, or a random act of kindness. The process of showing gratitude is not only about including others...it's also about being thankful and conscious of the positive aspects of your current life. You may not be exactly where you imagined yourself to be after forty, but being thankful for your current situation can reduce negativity and stressors in your life. Showing gratitude allows you to focus less on what's lacking and appreciate more of the blessings you enjoy every day.

Make it a habit to show gratitude daily. Schedule time once a day to either show gratitude to someone else or to simply give thanks for your current journey. There's no right or wrong way to give thanks. I spend my morning commute to work as time to give thanks and show gratitude. Focus your thoughts and channel your energy towards positive things. If you need a little help getting started, you can Google numerous blogs and watch various motivational speakers on You Tube to find tips on how to show gratitude. Don't get engulfed in how long it should take or what to say. There's no right or wrong way to do it. Just reflect upon the positive aspects of your life. The more often you practice showing gratitude and being thankful, the less time you will have to spend complaining.

Tip: Gratitude cost you nothing and the returns are far greater than the investment.

30-Day Challenges – Upgrading your Perspective

Changing the way you think or seeing things from a different point of view can be difficult but it is essential to your personal growth and development. Try these 30-day challenges below to start the process of upgrading your perspective. Remember, the change you seek starts from within.

30-Day Self-love Challenge:

- Write at least one positive thought about yourself every day for the next 30 days.
- Make the positive thought exclusive of your job, career title, or material possessions you own. The thought should be about you as a person and as a woman.
- The thought can be simple or complex, but it has to about you.

Ex: I am very compassionate and loving.
   I have a beautiful smile.
   I love my positive outlook on life.

30-Day Love Thy Neighbor Challenge:

- Buy a box of Thank You cards or blank cards.
- Every day for the next thirty days, write one compliment or nice thought about someone else.
- It can be your neighbor, friend, significant other, child, parent, etc.
- It has to a different person every day for the next thirty days.

Ex: My husband is very compassionate and loving.
   My sister has a beautiful smile.
   I love my coworker's positive outlook on life.

CHAPTER 6

Reinvent Yourself

Now that you've gotten the ball rolling by upgrading your perspective, it's time to use your new and improved intellect to produce some tangible results. Your first challenge is to reinvent yourself. This is a much deeper endeavor than going out and buying a new outfit or getting a makeover at the local MAC Cosmetics counter. This reinvention involves a mental makeover that includes shedding your self-defeating behaviors, developing new habits, and setting new expectations for you and others around you. Remember that you are not the same person you were a decade ago, or even two years ago. So letting go of outdated beliefs and habits or prioritizing your goals differently than you did in your thirties is really not a bad idea.

During my thirties, my top priority was to physically empower women. My classes and my business values were geared towards physical fitness, loving yourself and being happy in your own skin. I focused on building confidence and nurturing my clients' self-esteem. But as I segued into my forties, those concepts were no longer enough. I wanted to transition to something different, something greater than my current self. I wasn't interested in entering a new field or starting a new business from scratch. I had to figure out my next move without reinventing the wheel.

Once I turned forty I decided to channel my energy and efforts in a new direction. I wanted my new persona to embody the many roles (not just the professional roles) that I hold in life, such as mother, grandmother, daughter, sister, friend, mentor, and author. I also wanted my next business platform to promote more than being physically fit and aesthetically appealing. After a few weeks of soul searching, I decided to focus my efforts on being fabulous after forty. I would focus on creating the life I wanted and help others do the same. This would be the best way to bridge the gap between my personal and professional personas.

But what exactly did "fabulous after forty" mean? What does being fabulous look like, sound like, talk, sleep and breathe like? The concept sounded great and offered lots of room to expand, but I wasn't quite sure of how to make the transition to being fabulous. I needed a new mantra, a new image. I needed to reinvent myself, but I didn't know how.

So I followed the lives other women who were successfully living Fit, Fabulous and Focused lives. Queen Latifah, Tyra Banks, and Gwen Stefani were all over forty and appeared to be in the best shape of their lives and careers. I read the biographies of Shania Twain, who recently returned to the music scene for her first tour in 14 years after a bitter divorce. Robin Roberts, co-anchor of Good Morning America, survived a very public battle with a rare illness in 2011 and returned in 2013 more determined and focused than ever. Paula Abdul made calculated moves at the age of forty and revived her career by becoming a judge on the insanely popular American Idol in 2002.

I was intrigued by Celine Dion's career, which didn't end after a three-year sabbatical from international performances. In fact, her popularity evolved after she gave birth to a son and returned to work. She penned a very lucrative deal with Caesar's Palace in Las Vegas. To date, she has parlayed her talents into a contract yielding $475,000 per show, performing 70 shows a year. Jennifer Lopez' power move is nothing to frown upon either. Though she only performed 20 shows in her Las Vegas residency at Planet Hollywood, she still garnered $350,000 per show. Not a bad after-forty reinvention.

After reading the stories and biographies of these women, I was motivated beyond words to reinvent myself. And I realized that I didn't have to limit myself—I could be Fit, Fabulous and Focused at the same time. The dilemma, however, was figuring out how to embody all three qualities successfully. Where would I begin? How would I start?

No worries. I took a deep breath, pulled out my journal and favorite snack, and began to write. I was determined to write until I figured it out. My first stop: The Interview.

Interview Yourself

What better way to figure out who you want to be than to interview yourself? Get out a pen and a pad. I'm kind of old school and love to write, but if you prefer your iPad or laptop, I totally understand. Find a quiet spot, clear your mind and pour a glass of your favorite beverage. It doesn't have to be an alcoholic beverage. It just needs to be your favorite. Sip slowly and read the list of questions below out loud and answer them truthfully. After answering each question, read the answer out loud. Listen as you answer the question and make notes as needed. If there's any answer you want to revise, wait until you've answered all of the other questions before doing so. Treat the questions as real interview questions and give answers that reflect what you want to achieve or obtain.

Exercise #2

- Where do you see yourself in ten years? In twenty years?
- What did you want to be when you were growing up?
- What are your current short-term goals?
- What are your dreams?
- Are you happy?
- What makes you happy?
- Do you have any regrets?
- What do you want more than anything in the world?
- Do you want to be wealthy?
- Are you healthy? If not, what keeps you from being healthy?
- What will you do when your kids leave home for good?
- What do you like?
- What do you dislike?
- What are your fears?
- What are you grateful for?
- What is your favorite book?
- Favorite movie? Why?

- What do you want to leave as your legacy?
- What are you most proud of? Why?
- What is important to you?
- What motivates you?

It may sound a little silly, but asking these questions (and a few others) is key to getting reacquainted with yourself before embarking on the grand reinvention of your life. Interviewing yourself helps you focus on your goals, develop a few new ones, and prepares you for your next power move. Don't rush to write the first answer that comes to mind. Give yourself ample time to think before answering the questions and feel free to change your answers as needed. Often times as women, we can answer these types of questions on behalf of our kids, spouses and other loved ones, but we frequently fail to know the answer to the same questions on our own behalf. If you plan to successfully recreate your self-image, knowing yourself is a critical piece of the puzzle.

Fall in Love with Your Flaws

If you frequent the Internet and engage in social media as often as I do, then it's easy to discover at least one new personal flaw per day since turning forty. There are so many tips and techniques on how to conceal your imperfections that it becomes next to impossible to accept or fall in love with them. We all have flaws and imperfections, and now that you are over forty, you are probably well acquainted with most, if not all, of them. Changing your focus is critical if you want to win at loving your flaws. You can no longer focus on your imperfections!

I am a huge advocate of loving the skin you are in and feeling good about yourself, but I'm an even bigger enthusiast of adopting a healthier lifestyle and getting in shape. Which, by the way, is a great way to redirect your focus and minimize your desire to fix your flaws. Don't panic! I'm not suggesting that you sign up for a gym membership or the next fitness boot camp at your local recreation center. Nor am I asking you to become a vegan or stop eating sweets. Adopting a healthier lifestyle simply means making healthier choices for your life. You can adopt a healthier lifestyle by exercising self-control and doing things in moderation.

You can make small decisions such as substituting water instead of drinking soda or eating nuts and fruit instead of chips and chocolate. Add a little cardio to your day by taking the stairs at the office or jumping rope after work. Try power walking from one end of your building to the other during your lunch break. Don't eat at your desk for lunch and stay away from the vending machines in the cafeteria. Get a hobby. Go swimming or learn to swim. Eat breakfast. Sit up straight to improve you posture. These small changes in your daily activities may not yield significant improvements overnight, but they will make a huge impact over a period of time.

As you embark on your journey to create the life you want after forty, you must challenge yourself to fall in love with your flaws. The media will continue to seize every opportunity to bombard you with images and jargon that make you feel like altering, changing, getting rid of, or enhancing something about your uniqueness. Your countermeasure to this constant pressure is wisdom. At the age of forty, I became very familiar with the serenity prayer:

God, grant me the serenity to accept the things I cannot change, courage to change the things I can, and wisdom to know the difference.

Rely upon your wisdom to get beyond the altered, airbrushed images. Reject the reality show misrepresentations of women that bombard your world every day.

Here's my personal list of tips to help you fall in love with your flaws:

- Graciously accept a compliment without a rebuttal.
- Stop explaining your past.
- Laugh at your mistakes.
- Share a personal testimony without worrying what others will think.
- Know how to accentuate your best physical asset.
- Confidently enter a room full of people by yourself.
- Show affection to your significant other or loved ones in public.
- Know what makes you happy without the help of others.
- Hang out by yourself every now and then.
- Be genuinely happy for someone else.
- Be yourself all the time.
- Be yourself without making others uncomfortable.
- Give and take constructive feedback without damaging your relationships or feeling insecure.

Become your own Brand

Becoming your own professional brand goes beyond a well-written resume and a handful of business cards. Your brand is a culmination of your various professional talents, your personality, and the professional identity you create in the minds of others. Your brand is not limited to the position or title you hold and should be based upon concepts such as 1.) your successful reputation for consistency and satisfactory performance, 2.) visible and distinguished recognition in a particular field, 3.) credibility and desirability as a subject matter expert, and 4.) your personal vision or mission statement.

When I moved to Jefferson to start my new job, I had a clear vision of what I wanted my brand to be. I wanted others to recognize me as a powerful executive who exuded confidence and sophistication. I wanted to look as important as I felt and empower and inspire others. I knew that my vision would require me to look professional and marketable at all times. Therefore, I needed a wardrobe change among other things. My professional wardrobe was far too "business casual" to represent my new brand, so I decided it was time to do a little shopping.

And I was also going to need another car. Yes, my car needed an upgrade too. My 1995 Saturn didn't particularly scream confident, sophisticated executive. The majority of my thirties was consumed by my matriarchal role in my family, which my car definitely reflected. So I bought a new vehicle that would help me look the part as I strove to develop my own marketable professional brand. I continued to revamp every aspect in my life until I was visibly distinguished from others.

Once you identify and visualize your brand, it's time to take the next step. This means projecting your brand in everything you do. Attend meetings or host functions that allow you to propagate your brand. If you are a hairstylist or colorist, visit hair shows or host style camps to showcase your talents to other stylists. Establish your presence in the business community by attending networking functions at the local Chamber of Commerce or at business mixers. Expand your brand by volunteering for projects that coincide with your personal vision. (We will discuss personal vision in more detail in Chapter 10). If you're a health care professional, volunteer to work special events like an annual cancer walk. Consider donating time to organize a health fair for women over forty, or become an ambassador for other causes near and dear to your heart.

As you establish your brand, maintain consistency and continue to build on your strengths. Expand your social network. Make your presence known!

Get a New Job

Why do you stay at your current job when it makes you unhappy, bored, and unsatisfied? Why do you agree to be underpaid? Why would you even consider putting up with this misery until retirement? I realize job hopping is not preferred from the employer's perspective, but this section was written for the employee, not the employer. If your job no longer fits, then make a plan to quit! Stop trying to make the position you've outgrown continue to fit your life. It impedes your personal growth and development.

Yes, there may be risks involved with taking a new job. There is possible uncertainty in giving up your current comfort zone. There's also fear and anxiety as you step out on faith to quit your job or start a new career. But think of the alternatives: no longer waking up to a job you hate, going to work unhappy everyday, and gaining much desired growth and development. If you are already in your forties, do you really want to spend the next twenty years being unhappy simply because you are afraid of stepping outside of your comfort zone?

Let's look at it from a different angle. If you remain in your current position doing a job you hate for twenty-five more years and only work a forty-hour work-week, you would spend 52,000 more hours of your life feeling miserable and unhappy. This is assuming that you have planned well enough to retire at sixty-five!

As you search for a new position, don't forget to consider temp-to-perm assignments and contract positions offered by the local staffing agencies. Ensure that you communicate to the staffing agency that your decision to accept a lower paying or contractual position is only temporary. Your ultimate goal is a permanent, full-time position. Work diligently in the temporary position and establish a rapport with the hiring agency.

Make it a process to follow up weekly with not only this potential employer, but with others as well. Designate a specific morning for follow up phone calls, "keep me posted" emails, and personalized thank you letters. Courtesy and follow through are two of the most important aspects of facilitating a successful job search.

Start Your Own Business

If you already have talent in a specific area, consider capitalizing on it. Turn hobbies into cash. Baking, photography, music, coaching, pet sitting, professional organizing, and dance instruction are just a few hobbies that can bring in extra money during periods of unemployment. You may not make enough to sustain your current living expenses, but at least you'll produce some income. Once you find a full time position, you can continue your "paid hobbies" as a part time venture.

Start small and expand upon your idea. A few inexpensive business cards and an economical website template can give you the accessibility, appearance, and professionalism of a thriving small business, even if you are a one-person operation. With inventory management options such as drop shipping and payment collection options such as PayPal and the Square, the opportunities are endless for online businesses.

Professional Licensing

If starting over or changing careers is not in your reinvention plan, try advancing your current skill set with a professional license. These certifications compliment your current educational and professional status and often warrant additional income. Reinventing yourself doesn't always require you to go back for a bachelor's or master's degree. Consider becoming a real estate agent or a project manager. Sign up for continuing education at a local university. You may have always wanted to become CPR and First Aid certified, but had no clue where to start. Many YMCA locations offer these life saving courses, which can be invaluable on the home front as well as in the office.

Apply for internships and co-op programs. Volunteer to gain experience. Become an understudy or find an apprenticeship program. Likewise, you may be inspired to pursue a life long interest in American Sign Language. There are many low-cost courses on sites like Udemy that provide instruction and a certificate upon completion. The same goes for graphic design, website development and novel writing.

30-Day Challenges – Reinvent Yourself

Reinventing yourself can be a fun and rewarding experience. Let the 30-day challenges below help you change the way you see yourself and move beyond your comfort zone.

30-Day Clean up the Clutter Challenge:

- For the next thirty days, spend time making your home happy by removing clutter.
- Spend thirty days clearing out anything that you have not used within the past three months.
- Discard or shred any magazines, receipts, medicine, food, and vitamins that are beyond their expiration date.
- Donate any clothes, make-up, perfume, jewelry, old electronics, and shoes that you have not worn or used with the past two years.
- If you can't declutter your home in 30 days, break the task into areas such as the bedroom, the kitchen, and the family room. Tackle one area every 30 days.

30-Day Recycle Your Wardrobe:

- Choose ten outfits from your current wardrobe. Challenge yourself to make each outfit noticeably different the next time you wear it.
- You may use your current earrings, purses, shoes, leggings, hats, hosiery, scarves, jewelry, nail polish, makeup, and hair accessories to accentuate the outfit.
- You must wear the recycled outfits again within the thirty-day period.

30-Day Embrace New Technology Challenge:

- Identify one aspect of technology or social networking that you do not use (i.e. Bluetooth, Talk to text, Instagram, Twitter, etc.).
- Use it avidly for the next thirty days.

30-Day Gain a New Skill to Add to your Resume:

- Attend a continuing education class, seminar, or on-the-job cross-training opportunity within the next thirty days.
- Thoroughly familiarize yourself with this new skill during a thirty-day period.
- Add the new skill to your resume.

> *"Train yourself to let go of the things you fear to lose."*
> ~ GEORGE LUCAS

CHAPTER 7

Believe That You Can

J.K. Rowling, author of the Harry Potter series, has sold more than 400 million copies of her books. Seven years after graduating from college she became a divorced mother of one, was jobless, lived on state benefits, and was diagnosed as clinically depressed. Her manuscript, *Harry Potter and the Philosopher's Stone*, was submitted and rejected twelve times before she was accepted by a publishing house in London and received a $1,500 advance. Today J.K. Rowling is the 197th richest person in the United Kingdom. She is the UK's best-selling living author and has a net worth of $600 million dollars.

Viola Davis is an Emmy winner, Golden Globe winner and Oscar nominated actress known for her roles in the movies "Doubt," and "The Help." She is the lead actress in the hit primetime series "How to Get Away with Murder" and co-starred with Denzel Washington on Broadway in the play "Fences," for which she won a Tony award. During recent interviews, Davis described how she overcame extreme poverty and hunger as a child. She recalled being so hungry that she stole food and jumped in garbage bins with maggots to get food. Despite many obstacles, she graduated from Juilliard and was the first African-American to win an Emmy for Outstanding Lead Actress in a Drama Series in 2015.

Singer and songwriter Shania Twain has sold over 85 million records, received five Grammy awards, and has stars on the Hollywood Walk of Fame and the Canadian Walk of Fame. Shania started singing in bars at the age of 8 to help her family pay bills. Although she hated singing in bars, she loved music and was able to write her first song at the age of 10. As her singing career progressed, her parents were killed in a car accident. She put her career aspirations on hold and moved back to her hometown to take care of her younger siblings. After they graduated high school, she focused on her career again and garnered unprecedented success as a country singer. She was recognized as the best-selling female artist in the history of country music. In 2010, Shania experienced a publicly humiliating divorce from her husband of 15 years, and also suffered from a vocal cord condition called dysphonia. In 2015, Shania announced that she was going on tour for the first time in 11 years.

What do all of these women and their stories have in common? They are women over forty who are Fit, Fabulous and Focused. They've all endured hardships to create the life they want. Despite obstacles and temporary setbacks, they all believed in themselves and didn't give up on their dreams and goals. They were relentless in their quest for happiness and are still going strong today! Their stories can resonate with women of all ethnicities and walks of life.

As I wrote this chapter of the book, I quickly realized it would be the most pivotal. Why? Because the remaining chapters are about taking action, including "Creating a Vision Statement," "Assembling Your Team," and "Asking for What You Want." But if you don't believe in yourself first before taking on these endeavors, your efforts will be in vain.

Creating the life you want after forty is not about following someone else's plan. It is about identifying your own idea of success and bringing it to fruition. Your idea of success may be raising a healthy and happy family, earning a six-figure salary, marrying the partner of your dreams, traveling the world as you please, owning your own business, or completing your education. It may be working contentedly at a full-time job and pursuing your hobbies. It may be retiring and enjoying your grandchildren. Creating the life you want is truly about believing that you deserve to be happy on your own terms. It's about your power to make better decisions. It's about choosing wisely for your future and using your experiences as stepping stones to take you to the next level.

In order to get to that next level or to achieve your next goal, you must first believe that you can. This concept does not always come easy to a lot of women. As I mentioned in Chapter Four (Managing Your Emotions), we tend to be "emotional creatures" and have lots of self-defeating behaviors to overcome. I dedicate this chapter to helping you "get out of your own way" and start believing in yourself. Believe that you can! The process begins by surrounding yourself with people who will cultivate, support and celebrate your journey to becoming Fit, Fabulous and Focused.

Build Positive Relationships

An essential element to developing and sustaining our personal power is to share and attract positive energy. We build positive relationships by utilizing networking opportunities and nurturing professional relationships. Exchanging ideas, information, and support not only enlightens us, but also creates connections to others for years to come.

Find a mentor or become a mentor to someone else. Mentoring is particularly important for women as we strive towards our next career level. Whispering at the water cooler and belonging to cliques is no substitute for hard work and loyalty. Resist the temptation to gossip negatively about female coworkers, or any coworker, especially to people in higher positions. Why? Because most supervisors have advanced by maintaining their dignity, decorum and discretion. Chatting frivolously about your coworker's performance or personal business is the least likely way to get promoted to the next level. Likewise, your chances for promotion skyrocket when you display leadership qualities, including the ability to mentor and be mentored.

Most importantly, don't allow your fear and insecurity in the workplace to dictate the relationships you build with others. It has been said that smart women don't compete...they collaborate. With this in mind, tailor your behavior to reflect the "boss" within. Envision yourself as a dependable, fair, balanced and inspiring leader who others want to emulate—and then embody those qualities.

Build relationships that are open-minded, authentic, available and supportive. It is important to reciprocate mutual effort and avoid undermining other female acquaintances. Accept their differences and encourage their efforts. Take a moment each day to compliment or spend time building a rapport with your colleagues and acquaintances. There is no one size fits all mold for personal relationships, so nurture each one individually.

Capitalize on Your Knowledge and Expertise

During your journey through your forties and beyond, you'll draw on a lifetime of accumulated wisdom. This wisdom can help increase your income and enable you to live comfortably—a top priority on your "after forty" To Do list. But first you must learn to capitalize on your personal power so that you can one day retire, relax and enjoy the fruits of your labor.

A traditional way of increasing income usually involves going back to college for an advanced degree or additional certifications which can lead to a better paying job. Those who do not wish to return to college may opt to work multiple jobs to achieve retirement goals (been there, done that)! Yet countless numbers of women miss a golden opportunity to generate income by simply turning a passion into a paid hobby or side business.

For instance, I know a full-time employee who makes adorable hats for her grand-children and never even thought of selling those hats to others...until someone invited her to a weekend craft show. She sold out and ended up taking orders. Today she supplements her income by catering to an endless supply of newborns and toddlers. Think about that! As long as women have babies, her customer base is assured. Better yet, after work she sews at her leisure while doing the same thing she'd normally do on her couch—watching TV. This paid hobby has changed her life.

Never feel guilty for charging for your services. Another friend of mine tutors students in the evening, and you can bet she requires payment. Whether its offering piano lessons, keeping books for a small business, writing for magazines or pet sitting for your neighbors, there is always something you can do that peaks your interest and lines your wallet. After all, you practically give your power away to corporations, organizations, friends and family members for free every day. It's time you view yourself as a fee-earning entity in your own community.

In other words, you are very likely a subject matter expert in your career field or possess an incredible natural ability. Your talent, your time and your effort certainly justifies a fee. Never, ever say," Oh, just pay me what you can," or "It's on the house." Enough with being kind, polite and broke! Know the value of your product or service and disclose it before you transact business. It's certainly okay to underbid your competitors, but it is never okay to sell yourself short. Do not diminish your expertise. Instead, capitalize on it!

Having the life you want after forty means getting beyond the misconception that you exist solely for the purpose of giving to others. Instead, try to visualize yourself as a "provider" to others—a supplier to those who need your services. You are powerful. You deserve compensation. This does not make you bitchy or exploitive. Rather, it makes you a business woman who does not allow others to do the "exploiting." You should want more for your life. You deserve what you earn, and only those who seize opportunities can position themselves to get ahead financially.

If you begin to doubt or waiver in your quest to capitalize on your knowledge and expertise, please remember:

- People will pay for what they value.
- You can never get back the "free" time you've given away.

Minimize your Weaknesses

The thing about weaknesses is that we all have them. Just because you focus on overcoming your weaknesses doesn't guarantee they will go away, so it's important that we put things into perspective. Our weaknesses may not be the earth-shaking deal breakers we perceive them to be.

We live in a world that glorifies perfection, but reality proves otherwise, right? No one is perfect and everyone has flaws, both personal and professional. Once you identify that you have a weakness, dig a little deeper to understand the ramifications. Ask yourself if a weakness is holding you back. Will fixing it improve your life or your vastly accelerate your career? Will overcoming the weakness actually matter in the scheme of things? If not, then your goal is to simply minimize your weakness so that your assets shine through.

You may feel you have a weakness just because you are surrounded by others who are better at a particular task. It's not the end of the world, because you very likely excel at other tasks. In other words, your strength balances your weakness. My boyfriend, Richard, is a prime example. He is an incredibly talented artist and architect who can bring any canvas, mural, or home interior to life with minimal effort. But technical tasks are not his strong suit, so I manage the website content, e-commerce and brand recognition for his online art gallery (www.raartpublishing.com). Now I, on the other hand, am absolutely terrible with a paintbrush and have never successfully painted a wall without ruining the ceiling. Needless to say, Richard takes care of paint projects because I have neither the time nor desire to improve my home décor skills. But together we still produce an impressive and desirable outcome.

My point is that "partnering for results" is an effective way to minimize weaknesses. Try leveraging your strengths by sharing knowledge, networking, building a strong support system, and finding ways to offset the "negatives." Further, merging your strengths with your passion creates unlimited opportunities for you to draw attention to your "positive" attributes.

Don't waste valuable time and energy trying to correct a weakness that isn't relevant. Ask yourself if your weakness can be easily overcome. Will the time, energy and effort required to overcome it make a difference in the long run? If not, focus your energy on developing your natural talents and strengths, which is really what matters in the grand scheme of things.

Showcase Your Strengths

Yes, it's okay to toot your own horn loudly and often, especially if you expect to capitalize on your strengths. But be strategic in your efforts. Showcasing your strengths doesn't mean monopolizing every conversation with a list of your accomplishments. It doesn't involve bragging rights or one-upping everyone around you. It simply means that you are utilizing every available platform to thoughtfully market your positive attributes.

Perhaps you are currently "good" at singing, managing projects, styling hair, planning events, advertising, public speaking, cooking, communicating, etc. It will take practice, patience, and repetition to become "great" in your field. You can achieve greatness by taking full advantage of opportunities as they cross your path. In other words, leverage your strengths by showcasing what you excel at whenever possible so that you can achieve desired results.

Make a list of the strengths that come naturally and that you utilize most often. Which of those strengths help you thrive, make you feel strong, or make you stand out? Which ones are you truly interested in or passionate about? Which strengths require minimal effort? Do you have a strength or skill that is in demand? If so, build evidence to showcase your strengths and seek positive written feedback from your peers. If you have a business or a website, post customer testimonials and add comments. Highlight news articles and other press that support your strengths. Display before and after photos of your work. Build a social media business profile and solicit followers so you can display future projects.

Let's say you're great at leadership and comfortable speaking in front of a crowd. Why not monetize those strengths as a public speaker, trainer, coach, radio on-air personality, or mediator? Take it a step further and reach broader audiences by hosting webinars and posting You Tube videos.

Finally, as you showcase your strengths and make use of your personal power, resist the temptation to do too many things at once. Be realistic about adding skill sets when you are already juggling multiple balls in the air. There are only so many hours in a day, and it's better to be a "master" at something than a "Jack of all trades." So embark on your journey toward greatness by first identifying what you excel at and love, and position these strengths so that others will notice.

Trust Your Gut

Call it a hunch, instinct, intuition, inkling, or a gut feeling...the name really doesn't matter. Just don't ignore the "nudge" when it happens! If there's ever a time when you should listen to yourself, it's when your inner voice signals you to take a second look, pay closer attention, or make a leap of faith. How many times have you suppressed your intuition because of a past experience or the fear of failure? How many opportunities have you missed due to self-doubt or an unwillingness to trust yourself?

Often times, especially in personal relationships, women forego their better judgment when facing uncomfortable or difficult decisions. This may involve staying in an unhealthy relationship rather than walking away. It may involve remaining silent during an opportunity to speak up. Have you backed away from sharing ideas, asking for a raise, or quitting a great paying stressful job to pursue a dream? In hindsight, you would have been better off acting upon your instincts. So if your inner voice tells you to co-parent rather than get married, listen! If your instinct is pointing you north, then don't go south. Ignore the unsolicited opinions of others during your decision making process. It's your life to live, not theirs, and you are ordained to act in your own best interests.

Be flexible. What works for you today may not be in your best interest tomorrow. Even if your last endeavor, deal, or venture was successful beyond your wildest dreams, there's always more to discover. Treat every interaction with others as an opportunity to learn something new. Schedule time for exploration, and it doesn't have to be through formal institutional channels. An audio book, a women's retreat, or a flurry of Google browsing may plant a seed that will blossom in the future. Be open to the "new," and trust your gut.

30-Day Challenges – Believe that You Can

With so much going on in your daily routine, it's easy to unknowingly incorporate doubt an uncertainty into your psyche. Try the 30-day challenges below to redirect the negative energy you encounter throughout your day.

30-Day Negativity Fast:

- Avoid words with contractions for 30 Days.
- Remove words like don't, can't, won't and shouldn't from your vocabulary for 30 days.
- Rephrase your thoughts to convey the same response without using negative contractions.
- Instead of saying "I don't want to go," try saying "I would prefer to pass at the moment."

30-Day Visualize your Success Challenge:

- Spend at least 30 minutes every day visualizing your success at something you want to achieve.
- Imagine every aspect of your success as if it was your 15 minutes of fame.
- Get lost in the moment and utilize all of your senses.
- Imagine what that glorious moment will feel like, what kind of day it will arrive on, what will you wear, who will be around, and what sounds you will hear in the background.
- Write down those thoughts every day.

30-Day Positivity Challenge:

- For the next 30 days, try to only think positive thoughts and focus on a positive outlook.
- Whatever happens, you will see the good side and discover positive "take aways."
- No criticism, complaining, or negative commentary can be spoken aloud for 30 straight days.

CHAPTER 8

Take Control of Your Finances

I know, I know. This concept was a tough one for me too, ladies, and I'm an accountant! So I can only imagine what tackling this concept is like for non-accountants. But if you're serious about having the life you want after forty, then you must learn to become fiscally fit. It's time to take control of your finances.

Before you get overwhelmed, lose interest or skip this chapter because of the title, I want to clarify what I mean. I'm not asking you to take an accounting class or become the next Suze Ormond. However, I am asking you to be honest with yourself about your current financial state. I'm also asking you to get serious about creating a plan today that will put you in a better financial position in the future. It's not too late to create wealth for you to enjoy in your latter years.

This means:

- No more splurging on "fake it 'till you make it" designer handbags and shoes.
- No more opening "90-day same as cash" accounts that you won't pay back within the 90 days.
- No more planning holiday shopping sprees and financing Black Friday deals on your credit cards.

- No more keeping up with the Joneses, the Kardashians, or anyone else that causes you financial hardships.
- No more emotional spending sprees because "You only live once" and "You're too blessed to be stressed."
- Most importantly, no more saving the minimal amount (or not at all) because you don't have the discipline to save for your retirement.

If none of the scenarios above apply to you, bravo! Pat yourself on the back, as you are well on your way to managing your own money. However, if you are a forty-something-year-old Diva and you find yourself currently practicing at least one or more of these financial lifestyles, then now is the time to make every effort to take responsibility. There is no better time to get control of your bad habits.

Truthfully speaking, your financial evolution will take a realistic change of habits. Brace yourself for some butt-kicking discipline and a well thought out action plan. Otherwise, you will remain financially dependent upon your employer and live paycheck to paycheck for the rest of your life. You must acknowledge your challenges today and commit to a better future that includes a well-deserved retirement. This may seem a tad bit overwhelming, especially after forty, but it is definitely possible. That's why this entire chapter is dedicated to helping you get started on your journey.

Start From Where You Are

I think I spent most of my thirties living paycheck to paycheck. Some financial hiccups were avoidable and others were not. When I unexpectedly became a grandmother multiple times in my 30s, I was not interested in financial planning and saving for the future because the difficulties of just managing my thoughts from day to day were, at times, overwhelming. So taking control of my finances wasn't really on my radar.

But as time passed I managed to get beyond a few financial hurdles and settle into my new role as "Mimi." I knew I had to turn my finances around or suffer the consequences later in life. Now my dream was to one day depart the workforce, relax, and travel the world. But to do so, I had to reevaluate exactly how to fund my future retirement—the sooner, the better!

So I started with the end in mind and determined how to achieve my goals. After looking through a few old journals, I was reminded of two major Bucket List items: 1.) to own a boutique publishing company and 2.) to write self help books for women. I certainly had the passion for these projects, but passion alone doesn't generate income. To strike these items off my list, I would have to research the digital publishing industry and establish myself as a publisher. Likewise, I would have to muster the time and discipline required to write.

I rolled up my shirtsleeves and got busy, motivating myself with the thought of dream trips to South Africa and Dubai by the age of 50. After revising my budget, I took a part time job to clear up old debts and to get back to intelligently managing my income. Once I committed to turning things around financially and sticking to my plan, everything else just fell in place. Within a few months, I was no longer living paycheck to paycheck and saving for the future was definitely a priority again. All at once, I was in a position to invest in a publishing house. And it was easier to write without the distractions of financial worries, as well.

Saving is the New Spending

If saving money is a difficult concept for you, take baby steps. Start with saving small amounts like $15 or $20 each week and increase it over time. Maybe $20/week sounds like a huge amount, but think of it this way: if you cashed your weekly paycheck in twenty-dollar bills, then stacked those twenties and removed only one...would you miss it? You could also commit to saving a percentage of your income instead of a dollar amount. By using percentages such as 15% or 20%, your savings will remain constant over time regardless of fluctuations in your income. The truth is, you can survive with one less nail appointment and one less cup of coffee at Starbucks. You won't miss it, and a bit of sacrifice is one way to take those small steps toward saving.

Use Direct Deposit to ensure the savings process will happen even when you don't want to save. It may take a few pay periods to adjust to your new net pay, but I'm positive that you'll find you don't miss $25 per pay period as much as you thought you would. Increase the amount gradually. Don't rush yourself. The key is to save without utilizing or borrowing from the funds you've saved. It really isn't a true savings if you have to dip into your account every other pay period. If you start out with a large amount like $50 or $100 each month and find yourself borrowing from those funds often, then reduce your contribution to a more affordable amount.

I can't exclude women who prefer to deal with cash. If saving money via direct deposit or payroll deduction makes you uncomfortable and you have the discipline to pay yourself first, by all means do so! As you deposit your check each week (or bi-weekly), don't leave the bank without making a deposit into your savings account. I know that for some of you this method may be inconvenient, but I've encountered numerous women over forty who feel more in control and at ease when they are the ones making the actual deposits. Having actual cash on hand can also make you accountable and more aware of what you spend daily.

Take advantage of your company's 401k Plan. Invest no less than the matched percentage. For instance, if your company matches up to 5% of your income, ensure that you contribute at least 5% of your income to take advantage of the maximum benefit allowed. If you are not comfortable with mutual fund selection or have concerns about the market, request a one-on-one session with the financial representative of your company's 401k plan.

Maintain a separate savings account for emergency funds. Mixing your savings dollars with other household dollars can trigger temptation to spend now and replenish later. Once you've reached your goal for an emergency savings stash, repurpose that money to pay down your debts. You may be tempted to use the repurposed money to take mini vacations or to splurge on upgrading your current cell phone and cable package. But if you are serious about managing your money and becoming fiscally Fit, Fabulous and Focused, then the time is NOW to sacrifice for your financial future.

Finally, get excited about taking control of your financial future. It's not too late. Continue your savings regimen and maintain your scheduled deposits to your account. Congratulate yourself as you watch your savings grow!

Downsize Your Debt

Now is not the time to worry about what others think about your financial condition. It's no one's business if you trade your new luxury car for an affordable mid-sized sedan. If you are judged for making smart financial moves, then the people judging you are clueless and probably destined to work into their eighties. If they can't appreciate your financial intelligence, then why care what they think!

I drove a 1995 Saturn for eight years to avoid having a car payment. I disconnected my cable two years ago and I currently do not have internet/Wi-Fi service in my townhouse. The objective is to downsize and get beyond your current financial crisis. I know it may be a little embarrassing to downsize. But if you look at your finances realistically, you are downsizing your current lifestyle because 1.) you can no longer afford it, and 2.) you want to get ahead.

Contact your creditors and negotiate lower payments on your current debts. If you have severely delinquent balances or the creditor is seeking to garnish your wages, ask for a settlement of past due balance. Request a 50% settlement of the past due principal balance or a forgiveness of the total late penalties and interest. The goal is to reach an amicable and feasible agreement that will resolve the outstanding balance on your credit report.

Stay in control and be firm during your negotiation. Remember, only you know what you can afford to pay, not the creditor. Accepting unrealistic settlement terms from a creditor will only cause additional stress and further impair an already damaged relationship between you and your creditor.

Get your settlement agreement in writing before you accept it. Make sure you read the settlement and check your budget thoroughly to make sure the payments are feasible. If you find that the settlement is not feasible, do not accept it. Respond to the creditor with a counter offer that is acceptable for you. Despite what the creditor says, you are not "required" to accept an offer. Keep in mind, both parties want to resolve a delinquent balance and there is usually room for negotiation.

The best part is that downsizing can be done within the comfort of your own home. Unless you broadcast your business to family and friends, no one will know of the payment arrangements, collection agreements, settlements, or other financial agreements you've made with your current creditors. You can downsize even more by renting a smaller apartment, getting a roommate to cut expenses and reducing your credit card limits. Believe me, there are far more people on the planet, including the Joneses and the Kardashians, who have downsized, and they are doing just fine.

Pay Your Bills

Establish good payment habits by paying your creditors and your utilities on time. Pay $20 extra every month on the principle balance whenever possible. If you can afford it, pay a full additional payment to the principle to expedite the repayment of the balance. Be careful about paying extra payments on the principle if you are on a tight budget. The goal is to live within your means as comfortably as possible without overextending yourself and dipping into your savings. If paying extra isn't possible in your current status, then make a plan to pay extra in the future. If paying bills is really not your forte, then follow the tips below to help simplify the task.

Choose a designated place for your bills each month. It doesn't have to be a mail holder in your home office. It can be as simple as placing a small bin on a counter so that all bills will be kept together. You can apply the same concept to the bills you receive electronically. Create a folder in your email inbox for bills and store them in that folder as you receive them via email. Being organized really helps you pay consistently, and on time.

Open all your bills and process the payment immediately. This prevents you from opening the bill and placing it back into the bin to "pay later." You can stay ahead of your bill payments by making a notation of what amount you will pay, the due date, and the date you made the payment. This can be a simple as circling or highlighting the payment amount and the date, and jotting down the date you paid on your calendar.

Establish a designated time and place to pay bills each month rather than leaving a trail of paperwork around your home. One of the most practical ways is to pay from your desk or whatever workspace you have in place. This allows you to establish a routine, keep organized, and develop the habit of paying your bills in a timely manner each month. Overall, you want to take the hassle out of money management so it does not overwhelm you.

Let technology work for you. Use your online bill pay service from your bank. The service is usually free and this allows you to plan ahead by scheduling your payments for the same date each month. You have complete control of this method, as most online banking services can be stopped or changed if needed before the next payment is deducted from your account.

Don't overcomplicate things or allow excuses to get in the way when it comes to paying your bills on time—or online. I've heard women say, "My husband takes care of the bills," or "He's the head of the household," or "I don't trust paying my bills online," or "I don't want anyone getting access to my bank account." The point is, you are a grown woman in your fabulous forties and perfectly capable of handling your own monetary responsibilities. It's time to get over your fear and take control of your finances. As the Nike slogan says, "Just do it!'

I really want you to be successful at achieving the life you want after forty, so don't let your fear of technology, a lack of commitment, or your traditional beliefs prevent you from learning to take control of your finances. Take it from me, a proud 45-year-old "Mimi" with five wonderful grandchildren—you never know when life will throw several unexpected financial curve balls your way. Be smart, be prepared, and be responsible.

Break Bad Habits

If you are currently living paycheck-to-paycheck or living beyond your means, taking control of your finances will be challenging. Temporary solutions such as borrowing money from your savings account (that you may not be able to replace) will only strain your current financial situation and encourage your already undesirable financial habits. It will be an even greater challenge to end those habits if you are unemployed or under-employed.

So what happens when you're no longer underemployed and you get that much needed pay raise, or you get that new job you've been anxiously awaiting? Like most Divas, you probably believe that it will be easy to break those bad habits as soon as you make more money. You may assume your income level will increase and enable you to meet your basic needs with ease.

Not exactly! What generally happens with most women I know is that their basic needs tend to expand as their income grows. Be careful that your "basic needs" don't suddenly include eating out, shopping, hair salons, dry cleaning, manicures, pedicures, spa appointments, girlfriend getaways and much more. You can easily be swept away by the availability of funds and slowly regress to the same bad behaviors that originally led you to live paycheck to paycheck.

The key to getting beyond the "fake it 'till you make, paycheck-to-paycheck, living above your means" lifestyle is to incorporate a few basic principles into your current financial status. When you see yourself slipping back into your old habits, revisit this list and regain your focus:

If you're making payments, you don't own it. You don't have to be financial wizard to understand this concept. Until you've paid the final mortgage payment, car note, or loan payment, the property belongs to the lien holder. If you feel the need to test this theory, try missing a few payments and let me know what happens.

Don't spend what you don't have. Lay-a-ways, travel packages, 90 days same as cash, payment plans, rent to own, and timeshares only obligate unearned monies and cause additional financial stress. Wait until you can afford to actually buy the item. If you commit your money to goods and services you are yet to receive, then you're only digging a deeper hole, especially if you're already in the hole. Trust me ladies, the item will go on sale again!

It's NOT okay to "fake It 'till you make it. This mindset is probably what got you in this predicament in the first place. When it comes to material things, "faking it" costs money. Fake handbags, jewelry, nails, hair, lashes, butt injections, collagen injections, rented rims, leased furniture, and smartphone rentals can easily amass to serious debt. Living faux is EXPENSIVE! Living fabulously means living authentically and with financial dignity.

Don't buy a home until you are ready. Buying a home is not just about the pride of ownership or an itemized tax deduction. Home ownership also involves the cost of maintaining it and your household appliances. When it comes to major purchases, don't forget to factor in the cost of maintenance plans and warranties, which can minimize abrupt, unexpected cost and prevent depleting your savings to pay for general repairs or unforeseen emergencies. Know the true cost of homeownership before you take the 30-year mortgage leap.

Bundled cable packages do NOT save you money. The average cable bill costs $134/month. That's more than $1,600/year. It is time to get over your TV obsession and reduce that ridiculous cable/satellite bill you've been carrying for years. You are probably watching only 15% of the 300 channels you have in your bundle package on a regular basis. You are paying additional fees to have cable access in every room and the ability to DVR shows on your television. Let's not forget the additional fees you are currently paying for deluxe cable access and the premium sports package. Stop locking yourself into these one or two-year package deals. Say NO to cable and try services like Netflix or HULU to cut down on your monthly expenses.

Stay away from title pawns and payday loans. Ladies, trust me, I know that times maybe "extremely tough" but title pawn and payday loans are not the answer. This is a vicious cycle of "robbing Peter to pay Paul." The interest rates and payments are designed to keep you in debt beyond measure. No matter how tempting or easy these loans appear to be, they can easily become an ongoing, sleep-losing nightmare if not properly managed.

Cosigning is NEVER an option. I know cosigning a debt sounds simple, and most close personal friends and loving relatives never intend to default. But it does happen more often than you think. Cosigning should not be taken lightly. It is more than simply signing your name on the dotted line. You are being asked to guarantee someone else's debt, and this means you are responsible for the payments if the borrower fails to pay. This includes Parent Plus loans and student loan cosigning. Think long and hard before you commit to cosigning on a long-term debt on behalf of your child or a niece or nephew. Be realistic about your ability to repay the debt if the student defaults on the loan or doesn't finish college. If the debt isn't repaid by the student, then you are stuck with the debt.

Ask a Professional

When it comes to major financial affairs of your household, seek professional guidance. You wouldn't allow your hairstylist to work on your car or ask your postman to repair your roof. So don't short change yourself by seeking advice from family and friends when it comes to your finances. Reputable financial planners and credit counselors provide guidance, support and discipline that you may not otherwise develop on your own. When you meet with the budget counselor or financial planner, be honest about your current status. Listen to suggestions even if you think you already know the answer. Remember, asking for help is a part of recovery. It is not a confirmation of failure. You may also want to try a home-based product such as Quicken or online banking to add structure and automation to your financial routine.

Review your financial priorities often. Your financial priorities at twenty-five will probably not be the same as your priorities at thirty-five and forty-five. Once kids and spouses are involved, your priorities will fluctuate even more. Other factors such as promotions, marriages, births, deaths, medical issues, and relocations may also cause a sudden shift in your financial priorities. Communicate changes to your partner and be aware of changes in his or her priorities as well.

Don't build your budget based on the salary you had or desire to have. Your budget should be a simple guide that allows you to pay your bills on time and live within your means. It is a tool a based on honesty (numbers do not lie) and should be based on your current financial situation. Build your budget realistically. Be truthful, be sensible, and be frugal.

(Exercise #3) Worksheet

Ladies, we all find ourselves in a financial bind from time to time. You may be tempted to acquire new debt or feel overwhelmed by a financial situation. Before you sign on the dotted line, sit in a quiet place (free from distractions and chaos) and answer the following questions. Read the answers aloud, wait 24 hours, and repeat the process. Then reassess your original decision.

Question: What's the absolute deadline to have the money in hand?

> Hint: Don't act emotionally. If you are borrowing money based on a final notice or final due date, call the creditor (more than once if needed) and ask if the final payment date can be extended.

Question: If you don't get the cash in hand, what's the worst that can happen?

> Hint: Sometimes how you "feel" about the outcome is actually worse than the outcome itself. Will there be a loss of life, will your lose your home, will you lose your car, your job, etc? No! Most "financial emergencies" can be managed and overcome if you keep a level head, communicate with creditors, and avoid making emotional decisions.

Question: Is borrowing the cash a matter of necessity, or is it to avoid discomfort?

> Hint: Carpooling, using public transportation, downsizing your apartment, canceling memberships or having a yard sale may be temporarily embarrassing and inconvenient, but in the long run these options are definitely worth the peace of mind (and the cash in hand). Don't solve a temporary problem or inconvenience by taking on new debt. Be creative and be patient. Find a way to manage your short-term financial crisis without making a long-term commitment for a loan.

Question: Are you able to acquire the needed funds through other means such as your church, family member, or public service organizations?

Hint: Ask your pastor or church counselor if temporary assistance is available. Ask if any public service organizations are your community that provide assistance based on financial need. Ask friends for advice and speak with others who may have experienced similar situations.

Question: If the debt involves a creditor, have you contacted them to discuss your options or make arrangements (even if you've broken the terms of your agreement previously)?

Hint: Call your creditors and explain your financial situation, especially if it has changed. When calling, offer alternative solutions that work in favor of both parties such as a postdated payment or bank draft from your account at a later date when funds are available. They may be willing to lower the interest of the loan, extend the terms, or accept interest-only payments temporarily until you get back on your feet. If you can afford it, offer a partial payment or a feasible lump sum final settlement in lieu of monthly payments.

Question: If you overcome the obstacle by acquiring more debt, what is the likelihood that it will occur again?

Hint: Remember, your goal is to STOP backsliding into old habits. If you fund a payment by acquiring a new debt, you may not be able to afford your current debt along with a new loan payment. You must break this vicious cycle.

"New Debt + Strained Finances = More Stress"

30-Day Challenges – Financial Freedom

Ladies, you can improve your financial fitness by maintaining your focus and making smart financial moves. The 30-day challenges below can help!

30-Day Fiscal Fast (A No-Spend Month)

- Plan ahead for your fiscal fast and sit tight during the tempting holiday months.
- Don't buy anything that isn't necessary to live for thirty days. If it isn't food, medicine, or gas for your car, don't buy it.
- Take your lunch to work. Cook breakfast and dinner. Eat meals at home on the weekends and go out for activities in between meals.
- No debit or credit cards or online spending. No impulse spending.
- Track your lessons learned and changes you'd like to make.

30-Day Challenge: Set the Record Straight

- Over the next thirty days, take a look at all of your current insurance policies, your Will, investment accounts, etc.
- Update your beneficiary information, distributions, and instructions.
- Print a copy of all documentation and put it in a safe, accessible place.

Remember, a true commitment to your budget and your financial goals is required to create the life you want after forty and get beyond your current financial behaviors. You can achieve your goals with sacrifice and commitment.

CHAPTER 9

What about Love?

L ike the chapter about physical fitness, I decided I couldn't write a book about being Fit, Fabulous and Focused without adding at least one chapter about love! After all, most women over forty spend a great deal of time hoping to find new love, reminiscing about past love, or trying to sustain current love. When it comes to the topic of love and relationships, I'm no expert, but I figure that I'm as knowledgeable as any reality TV star and as candid as any talk show host. So that's all the qualification I need to share my advice with you—just kidding, ladies! But I can speak knowledgeably in this chapter, as can many of you, because at this stage in life we've acquired some wisdom and quite a bit of experience.

I am currently in a long-term relationship with a wonderful man and count myself lucky. However, my expertise on relationships actually falls into the nontraditional category. It's kind of like a unicorn—beautiful and unique and a tad bit delicate. If there was a book about nontraditional relationships, my picture would appear in the long distance / dating older guys / blended family categories. That probably sounds a little unorthodox and slightly unorganized to you, but for me, it's perfect. Truly, my goal is not to write about love as society sees it and as the media portrays it. I wanted to write about the kind of love that may not fit any mold or meet anyone else's goals except your own.

I'm not guaranteeing that you will immediately find a new mate, but I hope to at least get you a little closer to finding your prince or princess charming in the near future. I hope that this section of my blueprint to being Fit, Fabulous and Focused will give some insight in finding love on your own terms—and perhaps opening your mind to new ideas and future possibilities for your love life.

As for my own love life, where do I begin? I've been dating the same man for eight years. After eight years, you may wonder why I still call it "dating." Well, my situation is, once again, untraditional. Up until two years ago, we lived together. Today, we live apart. We're still in a relationship, but no longer under the same roof. We live in two different cities, two hours apart, and only see each other on weekends and holidays. We each maintain two separate households, actually three, but have unlimited access to each other's living space. We have our own successful careers and support each other's goals and endeavors. We both have a genuine love for family and are very committed to blending our families as one. Although we don't share any biological kids together, we collectively have four children between the ages of 18 and 30. We also have ten grandchildren.

We take vacations and attend events together. We get along with each other's extended families very well. We both work equally hard to create balance and share quality time with our friends and families. We live pretty active lives and do all the things most couples do—with the exception of physically being together during the week.

So why do we choose to bypass marriage and forgo the typical rules of a traditional relationship? It's because we both understand the power of choice. We choose to live this way. We are not driven by societal "norms" or anyone else's idea of what our relationship should be. We define our own success and work at happiness, both as individuals and as a couple. When Richard and I first started dating several years ago, we both struggled with the traditional roles of a relationship. I struggled with the idea of having more kids because my only daughter was already an adult when I met Richard. I even had two grandchildren when we met. He struggled with the idea of remarrying after experiencing a long marriage and a lengthy divorce. He already had three children and welcomed the idea of having more kids. So where did that leave us?

It left us in that unorthodox and unorganized space I mentioned earlier. Even though we didn't agree on the traditional concepts of marriage and children, there were so many other wonderful things we loved about each other and our relationship. Our chemistry was awesome and we truly enjoyed each other's company. Neither of us wanted to take the all-or-nothing approach and forgo our relationship because it didn't fit the mold of a 'traditional' relationship. After a few tweaks and adjustments, and some conversation and understanding, we agreed to meet in the middle. No new kids and no new marriage, just blending the families we already had and watching them grow.

It was, indeed, the art of compromise. And guess what? It works beautifully! We used the power of choice to define what is successful in our relationship. It works because we choose to make it work every day by staying active in each other's lives via text messages, phone calls and emails, and by making our time count when we're together. We have both learned to live in the present moment. Will our idea of a successful relationship change in the future? Perhaps. But this beautiful unicorn we've created together is what a successful relationship looks like right now.

The Art of Compromise

During my thirties, the common theme amongst my peers was becoming the ultimate independent woman. The movement was fueled largely by the blockbuster remake of Charlie's Angels in 2000. Their soundtrack featured the Grammy nominated, Billboard Hot 100 song "Independent Women" which held the number one spot for eleven weeks. Almost every up and coming thirty-something year old woman I knew was boasting and bragging about making her own money and calling her own shots. It was like a mini-revolution among women who were no longer willing to settle for less or compromise their dreams. Nothing about that song or the ideology behind it encouraged the art of compromise. Like my peers, I sang the lyrics proudly and blasted the melody from the speakers in my car radio. I considered myself a part of the movement.

As I approached forty, a few of my priorities and goals begin to change. I realized I had outgrown my "independent woman mindset" as I considered potential mates in both my personal and business endeavors. Suddenly, it wasn't all about "me." Oh, I still made my own money and called my own shots, but was ready to partner with a significant other. I was ready to compromise, and discerned that compromise did not mean settling for less. It was about letting go of something in order to gain something greater. Compromise is essential in building and sustaining successful relationships, and more often than not, it's not always 50/50.

Luckily I was not too far gone in the independent women's movement or too set in my ways to incorporate a little compromise into my love life. The process wasn't easy, and being open to compromise was an acquired skill set. At times I found myself firmly standing my ground and delaying progress on the simplest issues in our relationship, only to end up compromising later and gaining a win/win result. It was about growth, grace, love and commitment on the deepest personal level, in a way that was customized exclusively for me and my partner.

Reset your Relationship Expectations

Before you decide to compromise in the name of love, take a moment to review and reset your relationship expectations, in particular, your expectation of others. Ask yourself if you are setting your expectations too high or too low. If you've experienced failed relationships or find yourself repeatedly unhappy and involved with the wrong person, take a break from dating and evaluate your current expectations and behaviors about dating.

For instance, are you constantly comparing your relationship to someone else's, like a co-worker, friend or family member? If so, remember that you are not a clone! Your relationship will be, and is supposed to be, different than anyone else's. Or are you incorporating too much reality TV show advice or too many Facebook comments into your love life? Hopefully not, because virtual reality is no substitute for the joys and challenges of authentic conversation and real life interaction. Perhaps you are you holding on to a few unhealthy philosophies, such as believing that having a bad relationship is better than no relationship at all. I hope this is not the case, because Fit, Fabulous and Focused women love themselves enough to never settle for less than a healthy relationship.

Or do you believe that your new mate will change an undesirable behavior if he/she truly loves you? Ladies, we aren't magicians, and our powers to "makeover" our mates is limited. Maybe you've always believed that if you treat someone like you want to be treated, they will "always" reciprocate. Unfortunately, not everyone appreciates or follows the Golden Rule, and your responsibility is to weed out those who cannot or will not treat you well. Or do you believe that after being with your mate for a period of time, you shouldn't have to tell him/her how you feel because they should instinctively know? Well, guess what? The lines of communication are a precious thing, and you honor your mate by communicating truthfully, honestly and appropriately—and vice versa.

Perhaps you thrive on being the self-proclaimed "Ride or Die" chick who is undeniably loyal to her partner under any circumstances including infidelity and physical abuse. You may even tolerate a few misdemeanors and illegal activity in order to prove your love. None of these are healthy situations and are definite indicators that you have lowered your relationship expectations to the lowest level. You owe yourself so much more! Stop accepting less than you deserve.

There are several other unrealistic relationship expectations that women hold on to as they journey toward finding true love. Believe me, I've heard more than my fair share during my years of running a dance studio. There were times I simply embraced some-one who needed a shoulder to lean on. Other times, someone's personal beliefs were so unbelievable that I wanted to sound a secret buzzer and say "Bzzzzzttt...wrong answer!"

What I've come to understand on my journey to becoming Fit, Fabulous and Focused is that we are ultimately responsible for our own happiness. We are respon-sible for communicating to others what that actually means, and this includes estab-lishing expectations. Don't leave it up to your partner or your potential mate to figure it out for you. They may get it wrong and your lack of communication acquiesces consent. Resetting expectations doesn't guarantee you a foolproof relationship, but you can certainly save yourself a whole lot of heartache, not to mention a few head-aches, by remembering this critical step in your quest to find love. Feel free to use a few or all of the tips below to help you reset your relationship expectations and find the soulmate that you deserve.

1. Communicate your current expectations to your partner periodically. However, this is not an excuse to nag your partner into submission. Don't expect him or her to remember what you mentioned when you first started dating.
2. Don't play by the same rules that were applicable in your last relationship and hope for a different outcome. Remember doing the same thing over and over and expecting a different result is the definition of insanity!
3. Let things happen organically. Rushing your relationship to the next level by assigning titles, becoming intimate, and meeting each other's children is a clear indicator that you should pump the brakes and clear your head.

Make Room for Love

This topic is for those ultimate achievers—the accomplished, always on-the-go, got-to-make-it-happen Divas who have little to zero time or space in their hectic schedules for love. It's also for those "I've been single so long, why bother" chicks. And I can't leave out those "I sleep with my dogs and cats in my ex-boyfriend's t-shirt" chicks. In each of these scenarios, there is a common thread. None have made room for love in their lives. Whether it's due to a scheduling conflict, a lack of motivation, or being stuck in a rut, all of these reasons can keep you from making room for love.

It's time to stop making excuses and hanging on to the past. When it comes to love, new relationships are all about fresh starts. During my twenties, I remember spending the day watching movies on Lifetime about women who met their soulmate in the produce section at the grocery store, and women who bumped into the love of their life while working out at the same gym. Needless to say, that didn't happen to me. By the time I turned thirty, I remember working full-time, running my studio part-time, and juggling dates with male suitors who for one reason or another didn't hold my interest long enough to become anything more than dates. It wasn't until I consciously decided that I was tired of the dating scene that I was finally ready to make room for love.

That's when I finally met Richard. Prior to him, my love life mainly consisted of climbing the corporate ladder, working from sun-up to sundown, eating fast food on the go, and hanging out with male acquaintances to pass the time. I had to "make room" in both my professional and personal life so that Richard could enter, but I can't take any of the credit. It was actually Richard who showed me how.

It was a few years ago and I was wrapping up what had turned out to be a very long Saturday. After working all day hosting parties and classes until 8pm, I received a phone call. It was Richard. He chatted for a moment and wanted to know if I was leaving the studio soon. I told him yes, but only after I cleaned up first to ensure the studio would be ready for classes on Monday. We hung up and I proceeded to sweep and mop the floor. About 20 minutes later, my cellphone rang again. It was Richard. I said "Hey baby, what's up?" He said that he was just calling to check on me and wanted to know if I had left yet. I answered "no," with a heavy sigh. "I'm almost done. I have to lock up and I will leave in a few." By that time, I was slightly annoyed because my commute to get home from the studio was at least twenty minutes and it had been a really long day. So I locked up the studio, headed downstairs to get in my car and the phone rang again. It was...Richard. I didn't even say hello, I answered "Baby, I'm in the car... I'm on my way. You know where I am, is everything okay?" He said in a very calming tone, "I'm waiting for you. I'm making dinner and I wanted to know exactly when you left so that it would be ready when you got home. I didn't want your dinner to get cold."

I immediately stopped my car in the parking lot. His response was totally unexpected and a definite game changer. I had become so accustomed to eating on the go and eating alone that I barely remembered what a home cooked meal was. On top of that, I had forgotten the effort it took to prepare a delicious dinner, not to mention the courtesy that was expected when dinner awaited! Wow. I was so stunned that I didn't even have a response. I remember looking at my phone in disbelief, as if someone on the other end was offering me a prize. Never, ever had any man gone to that extent to make sure my dinner was hot. Never, ever had any man bent over backwards to ensure we dined together.

To put this in context, we both had pretty active social lives and he could've been in a million other places on a Saturday night, but he wasn't. He was at home waiting for me. Making time for me. Making room for us. I gathered my thoughts, which by then were total mush, and apologized for being so snappy. I told him I would be there in twenty minutes. Honestly, I don't even remember my drive home, but I do remember how my night ended!!!

What You See is What You Get

I've read blogs, social media posts and short stories about women who support their partner's potential, be it emotional, financial, or spiritual. I personally know several women who have stood by their partner's side through thick and thin because they have so much potential, only to find themselves weeks, months or years later full of regret for not ending the relationship sooner.

Why is that? Why do women find themselves in this predicament time and time again? It's because some women fall in love with a person's potential, but fail to realize they will be in a relationship with that person's reality. Women tend to envision all the things we want our partners to be, without knowing who that partner actually is. Our partners must "want" those things for themselves, and we cannot "will" this desire into existence. For instance, you may picture him/her making a six-figure salary while working for a company, or running his own successful business. You imagine him/her being a great parent to your children, as well as being a romantic and amazing lover.

But in actuality, your partner may not care to move up in a company. Your partner may be completely satisfied in a current position or circumstance. Your partner might have children from previous relationships with absolutely no intentions to have more. Your partner may not be physically well-endowed and has a small penis. Your partner may not like to cuddle or isn't the romantic type.

Pay attention ladies! What you see is what you get, and this is either a satisfactory reality, or it is not. Your partner isn't a clay mold that you can shape to your expectations. You cannot will or wish someone into becoming more than their potential. They must have the drive and willingness to do it for themselves. Oprah Winfrey shared one of her favorite life lessons, courtesy of the late poet Maya Angelou. She told Oprah "When people show you who they are, believe them the first time. When they say, I'm mean, I'm selfish, I'm crazy, I'm unkind...believe them. They know themselves much better than you do. You don't have to wait until the twenty-ninth time they say it to believe them." I think that is one of my favorite life lessons.

Second Time Around

When it comes to finding love, you may find yourself constantly reminiscing about the one that got away or secretly missing the one who still has the key to your heart. You may spend hours wondering what would have happened if you'd tried harder or had not given up so easily. Maybe you weren't exactly ready to call it quits and would like to try again.

Don't be embarrassed. This happens quite often. Breaking up with someone is not always because the person treated you horribly or cheated with your BFF. Relationships can end because one or both parties lack the emotional maturity to nurture and sustain the relationship. They can also end because you and your partner have different goals, expectations and priorities. People grow and things change. There may have been life events that caused a rift and you simply needed a break.

Whatever the reason was back then, you may feel that the relationship deserves a second chance right now. Becoming Fit, Fabulous and Focused is about learning to live in the present moment, right? So why not go for it. If you truly feel the two of you belong together and you're ready to put in the time, effort, energy and commitment it will take to make it work, why not give it one more try?

Try a Different Approach

Last but certainly not least, as you navigate your way to finding love after forty, get creative and try a different approach. Popular options like online dating and speed dating might be a great place to start. There are several well established online dating sites such as eHarmony, Christian Mingle, and Match.com to choose from. I don't have hands-on experience with any of these sites, but I personally know women who use them often. Online dating sites have come a long way since the first dating service, Match.com, appeared on the scene in 1995. Technology, accessibility and affordability has made online dating a preferred, inexpensive way to meet new people.

Living Apart Together (LAT) is the new terminology for long distance relationship. This is another creative approach to building a relationship regardless of your locale. I will be the first to say, long distance love ain't for everybody. It takes a Herculean effort to build a solid foundation, and establishing a routine under two different roofs requires massive amounts of communication. But it can work well for both parties if the commitment and desire is there. After the first year (yes, it took a whole year), Richard and I managed to find our groove. Finally, the concept of living apart felt less demanding and less chaotic. A word of caution about living-apart-together—don't expect it to be a 50/50 split with every decision you make. Compromise is the key!

Focused
(Follow One Course Until
Successful)

> The key to success is to focus our conscious
> mind on things we desire
> not things we fear.
> ~ BRIAN TRACY

n the pages ahead you'll learn how to create a vision for your life that will help you achieve your goals. But In order to fully execute your vision and achieve those goals, you must follow one course until successful. By focusing intently, we pay particular attention to things that truly matter. It took me a while to know how and when to focus, but today people will tell you that I "focus like a laser." I wasn't born with this talent—it's an acquired skill. The good news is that you can develop a laser-like focus of your own.

Think of it this way. We all were once students and know that focusing in the classroom was a proven way to achieve academic success. Most of us had extracurricular activities like music or volleyball, and we devoted intense focus to ensure we played well, or even competitively. So what about our present day journey? Doesn't the quest to be Fit, Fabulous and Focused after forty deserve our undivided attention and laser focus? Of course it does!

In our overly-distracted lives, it may seem impossible to shut off the diversions, interruptions and temptations that keep us off course. But once we develop habits for increased concentration and productivity, our focus sharpens and we are more equipped to visualize our goals...and achieve them.

Being focused involves creating a vision for our lives, adapting and overcoming, assembling a Dream Team, asking for what we want (and being specific), and last but not least, starting today! All of these topics are detailed in chapters below to uplift, motivate and guide you toward your dreams and goals. You can do this—follow one course until successful!

CHAPTER 10

Create a Vision for your Life

One of the most critical things I failed to do during the six years of having my own business was to create a vision. As I mentioned earlier in the book, I had a very thorough well-developed business plan, but my plan was only an overview of how my business should grow. It had financial projections, the description of the ideal location and the actual details of how I would run my day-to-day operations; however, my business plan did not provide purpose and direction on the next steps I should take. When it came to down to my next move, I can honestly say I was purely winging it.

I knew that my business deserved more than just "winging it," and ditto for my personal life. But at that point, I had never really identified what "more" would be. It's kind of hard to describe. Yes, I had a lot of activity in my life back then and anyone around me could clearly see that I was always busy. Since I've always associated busyness with progress, then I must've been making a whole lot of progress, right? Or was I really? Deep down inside, it sure didn't feel like progress. Instead, it felt like a whole lot of chaos and uncertainty. I had no idea of where my life was headed. It was totally scattered. I was a thirty-something-year-old 'busy-bee' with a little bit of this and a little bit of that going on. In fact, I had so much of "this and that" going on, I didn't know how to prioritize my focus. Very simply put, I didn't have a personal vision. This period in my life was challenging and could easily be summarized by the lyrics in the beautiful ballad by Diana Ross from the movie Mahogany, "Do you know where you going to, do you like the things that life is showing you, where are you going to...do you know?"

I didn't really begin to wrap my head around the concept of creating a personal vision until I turned forty. Yes, good ol' forty, that magic number. It seems like most of my A-HA moments and epiphanies happened in my forties. I just didn't realize how important the concept was until then. It coincided with a time when I had reached a standstill in my career and was contemplating keeping my old job and re-opening my fitness studio part-time versus looking for a new full-time job with more opportunities for growth and a better salary. I weighed the pros and cons of both options. I already knew that if I set the goal of re-opening the studio, I would achieve it. I also knew that my next studio would be bigger and better than the last one. I was excited about the possibilities. The nostalgic thoughts of days gone by and hanging at the studio until the wee hours of the night after a hard day's hustle were so enticing. I looked forward to the additional stream of revenue I would generate after spending all day on Saturday teaching dance classes and hosting pole parties. The memories were so awesome that I could hardly sleep at night as I imagined my eminent and grandiose return.

As I contemplated more possibilities, I decided to revamp my business plan and change the concept of the studio and the services I would offer. To get new ideas, I subscribed to numerous blogs and read books about achieving goals and pursuing dreams. I even read web postings about creating a personal vision statement. I thought, *Hey, this must be a new concept.* I'd worked in corporate America for several years and was very familiar with the concept of a vision statement for businesses, but I'd never heard of creating a personal vision statement for my life. The more I read, the more I was intrigued. The more I read, the more I understood that this was something I wanted to do. It was something I felt I needed to do, especially if I was going to open another studio. So I decided to create my very own personal vision statement. My personal vision would encompass all of my future endeavors, provide a sense of achievement, and make an impact wherever possible in the lives of women.

It didn't take long for me to decide that I would reopen my studio in a new location. I immediately began the process of locating a new spot. It had to have more square footage than the 800 square foot studio I previously operated. I also wanted minimal to no remodeling. When I rented my first studio, it needed EVERYTHING. It was an empty rectangular box with concrete floors and a small bathroom in the back left corner. No mirrors, no interior decor, it didn't even have a working telephone land line! I installed all of those upgrades and more. But I had no complaints because the rent was only $675/month, much less than I expected.

When I closed the doors at the old location, my lease stipulated that I couldn't take any of the improvements with me. They were legally a part of the unit and considered as Leasehold improvements. Leaving everything behind was difficult. It was heartbreaking and expensive, but I survived it and was now ready to try my hand again at opening another studio. As I searched for a new location, I knew from my previous experience with leasehold improvements that I wanted to lease a unit that required as little remodeling as possible.

After a few weeks of searching, I found a potential new location. I was so excited that I treated myself to dinner and a pedicure to celebrate the occasion. This new location was bigger and the rent was only $850 (a little more expensive, but still affordable). It was 1,200 square feet and already divided into two separate rooms. The bathroom was in the back of the unit and was large enough to serve as a dressing room. The previous tenants left the same type of wall displays that I previously used, so that was a plus for me. It had ample parking, but the parking lot was not as brightly lit as I desired.

Despite my efforts to avoid it, there would be some remodeling involved. The unit was carpeted, so I would have to install laminate flooring. I would also have to mount new mirrors and build a divider wall so my customers would have total privacy from the outside window. After careful consideration, I knew that I could make the changes for much less than I originally spent the first time around, so I proceeded with my plans to reopen. I felt a little uneasy about the remodeling process, but I simply treated those feelings as nervous jitters.

I contacted the leasing agent, visited the property a few times, and took measurements to determine the total investment required to get my new studio showroom ready. I was rolling full speed ahead. I visited a couple of pole dancing studios in Atlanta and researched market rates for dance instructors. I figured this time around, I would hire instructors and offer more classes. I updated my website, interviewed potential instructors and revised the class schedule in anticipation of the big day. Things seemed to be going great, but for some reason it didn't feel as good as I thought it would. It felt like I was going through the motions because they were familiar, but those previous feelings of excitement and eagerness had all but dwindled to checking off items on my grand opening to-do list. It seemed odd and I knew something was different this time around, but I just didn't know what that "something" was. This feeling continued as the days went by.

Late one night while finalizing the new concepts for the studio, I could no longer ignore that odd feeling. I couldn't shake it or move beyond it. Maybe it was merely my intuition, but the more I thought about it, the more it felt like an epiphany. Whatever it was, it was telling me that re-opening my studio was not the best move for me. This time I paid attention and listened to my inner voice. I couldn't put my finger on *why* I suddenly felt so differently about something I was so passionate about throughout my thirties. I just knew in my heart and mind that re-opening my studio was no longer what I wanted to do in the future.

Finally, it dawned on me. Opening another studio didn't align with my personal vision statement! I realized that my goals at the age of forty were different than the goals I planned in my thirties. The previous goals I accomplished were separate independent achievements in my life. They were goals that I randomly selected and typically centered on my own personal desires, like opening another studio. Now that I think about it, most of the goals I previously achieved were kind of on that same path. Once I achieved a goal, I was on to the next one. I reveled in checking off my goals on a bulleted to-do list and celebrating my moment of achievement before moving on to the next goal.

After reading about personal vision statements, I no longer wanted to achieve goals simply because I could or entirely for my own personal gain. I wanted to achieve goals that were tied to a greater purpose. I wanted to incorporate my beliefs and align my values with my future goals and spend the next phase of my life building and my legacy. I wanted to build my goals based on my vision for my life in my forties, and will do the same in my fifties and beyond.

My vision: To utilize my talents to mentor, inspire, and empower women one goal at a time by maximizing their full potential, improving their health and wellness, securing better financial positions, developing their spiritual relationships, and nurturing personal relationships.

Below is a roadmap that will help you create your own vision statement during your journey.

Distraction-Free Focus

It takes focus to build a bridge between the present and the future. We are highly prone to distractions, some more so than others, but the truth is, if you are sincere about getting focused, then you will find ways to cut back on the multitasking and friendly distractions that bombard you daily. These interruptions and disturbances greatly erode your ability to achieve your goals.

According to a study posted in the New York Times in 2013, it takes an average of 25 minutes to return to the original task after an interruption. You have your personal email, Instagram, Twitter tweets, and Facebook Messenger all set to alert you every time activity happens on your social media accounts. You have a work issued cell phone and office emails to manage, not to mention the personal text and phone calls you receive throughout the day.

You also likely have multiple tabs open on your computer desktop, a music app like Pandora running in the background on your PC, and a coworker dropping by to get your opinion or to give an update about a meeting you purposely didn't attend that morning. Then you head home with your blue-tooth connection securely in place to allow hands-free driving during an hour long commute. You enter your home and rush to the television to check your pre-recorded shows via DVR as you start dinner. Or you may rush off to one of the many sports activities involving your kids, only to wake up and do it all again the next day.

So where and how do we develop the discipline to focus on setting goals and achieving them? The key word—discipline—comes from an awareness that we are inundated with diversions. We must choose to give full attention to what matters and free ourselves from interruptions. Yes, you have to find the strength to temporarily disconnect and focus on the life you want and deserve.

If you've postponed your journaling, procrastinated on the creation of a vision board, or ignored the pursuit of goals, perhaps now is the time to shut down the distractions and concentrate on reconnecting to the larger picture—your grand plan of being Fit, Fabulous and Focused.

Begin with the End in Mind

Consider the quote, "Life is a journey, not a destination." It is true that we will all experience unanticipated twists and turns on our path toward being Fit, Fabulous and Focused. But the last thing we want is to find ourselves drifting aimlessly through life, and then wondering why we failed to achieve our goals. The purpose of our journey is to create the life we want, and taking paths that lead us toward our goals is both productive and sensible. We must have a clear idea of our destination.

Steven Covey's *The 7 Habits of Highly Effective People* suggests that we should always start things with a clear idea of our destination, so that the steps we take are always in the right direction. I truly believe that if I had not listened to my inner voice and proceeded with re-opening my studio, I might've spent years drifting farther away from my vision and other goals that were aligned with my vision, like writing this book. Maybe I would have eventually found my way back to honoring my vision, but there's no guarantee.

Creating a vision for your life (and honoring it) requires a lot of thought. It may take time to articulate your vision. You can reflect upon past and present life experiences as you work your way through the process. Once you start, you may find that you already have a vision for your life and just haven't yet written it on paper. There are several blogs on the Internet with thought-provoking questions that will trigger emotions and inspire thoughts to help you develop your vision. Keep in mind, there's no perfect formula or specific number of questions you must answer as you create your vision. If you don't answer all of them, that is perfectly okay. I've listed a few questions below to get you started.

Exercise# 4

- What do you want to do with your life?
- What matters to you most?
- What are you naturally good at? (skills, abilities, gifts, etc.)
- How do you want to be remembered? What legacy would you like to leave?
- Given your talents, passions and values, how could you use these resources to serve, to help, to contribute?
- What would you regret not doing, having, or being in your life?
- If you could get a message across to a large group of people, who would those people be? What would your message be?
- What do you love to do so much that I forget to sleep or eat?
- What kind of impact would you like to make on your community?

- If you never had to work another day in your life, how would you spend your time instead of working?

Dreams and Goals

Dreams and goals are both vital components required to carry out your vision. But they are two vastly different things. What I learned over the years about dreams is they don't have an expiration date. As long as you are physically and mentally capable of pursuing your dreams, you can. Whether you are in twenties or in your nineties, you can literally dream at any age. Dreams can inspire and motivate you to become better and greater than your current self. They can stretch your imagination to the fullest extent...and the best thing about dreams is they cost you nothing. Dreams do not require you to take action. You could literally spend your day or night dreaming for free. You can have multiple types of dreams. Career dreams. Financial dreams. Family dreams. Travel dreams. There's no limit to what you can dream.

Goals, on the other hand, do require action. Goals are basically the vehicle or the legs that allow you to achieve your dreams. Goals are achieved through effort, and often times a lot of it. Goals should be specific, measurable and also include timelines or deadlines for completion. All of the dreams you have written down in your dream book or on your vision board won't come to life without goals.

Goal setting deters procrastination, produces results and provides answers to context questions like who, what, when, where and how? Below are questions you can ask yourself about your specific goals.

Exercise #5

- **When** will you complete this goal?
  Is it a short term or long term goal? Is it a one-year or a five-year goal? Should you break this into smaller goals? Is this goal time-sensitive? How long will it take?
- **What** do you plan to achieve with this goal?
  A new certification, a new license. Business or home ownership. Monetary and financial gains, a degree, property, peace of mind, debt free, etc.?

- **Who** will complete this goal?

    Is this a solo effort or does it require multiple people? If so, who are those people? How many people will you need?
- **Where** will you pursue this goal?

    In your current location? Do you have to move? Do you need to lease a physical location? Can you do it from home? Does it require you to travel? Is this an online venture?
- **How** will you complete this goal?

    Do you have the resources, the skills, the time, and the money to do so? Do you need updated technology or additional tools?

Pursue your Passion Wisely

When I think about pursuing my passion, the term "opportunity cost" comes to mind. Opportunity cost refers to a benefit that a person could have received, but gave up, to take another course of action. In other words, we give up something to gain what we perceive to be a greater benefit.

For example, say you quit your full-time position as a partner in a law firm to pursue your passion for fashion. You open a boutique with your 401k savings and begin a new journey in a totally unrelated field. This an example of an opportunity cost—giving up the stability of a paycheck and benefits every two weeks, and letting go of a comfortable retirement in exchange for becoming your own boss and earning your living via the ups and downs of the retail industry. There's absolutely nothing wrong with that scenario, but it obviously has both negatives and positives.

I'm not here to discourage your efforts to pursue your passion, but I am here to encourage you to Do Your Homework first! Society does a great job of promoting the "pursue your passion" movement by painting a rose-colored romantic picture for those who are considering a huge professional or personal move. The average social media post may claim that quitting your job to do what you love or to start a new career is the new key to our happiness. Maybe? Maybe not? We are coaxed and tempted by the glamorization of transition. We are nudged to make bold, courageous and risky entrepreneurship decisions. Those who are brave enough to walk away from the stability of a full time job (and benefits) are celebrated. Those who opt for a 9 to 5 are treated empathetically as if their choice is less noble.

As a person who has ventured outside my comfort zone on multiple occasions, I learned a few lessons that are worth sharing. For instance, I strongly recommend that you "look before you leap," which is age-old advice that still holds true today. Before taking the emotional leap into pursuing your passion or becoming your own boss, try visiting the Occupational Handbook website (www.occupationalhandbook.com) to help weigh the pros and cons of your new field. A little research on this site could easily prevent you from overlooking the nuances, challenges and obstacles you might experience as you make your transition.

Again, "homework" is invaluable and I encourage you to think your plan through. By asking tough, honest and practical questions, you'll have a clearer picture of your future opportunities.

Exercise #6

- Are there positions in this field in your city?
- How will you supplement your income until your passion pays off?
- What is the average salary of someone in this new field with no experience?
- Can you afford a substantial pay cut?
- Have you networked with others in your new career field?
- Do you currently have clients or customers for your business venture?
- Do you have savings outside of your emergency fund?
- Is your spouse on board with your plan? If you pursue your passion, will your family's well-being or financial health suffer?
- Is there a market for your full time venture in your city or can you pursue your passion as a part-time opportunity?
- Do you have a contingency plan if things don't go as planned?
- Have you embraced the concept that your passion will not always make you money?
- Do you accept that your venture or passion may not always be glamorous? Will it require you to work longer hours? Will you have to work weekends or work on major holidays?
- Will you have to temporarily work an alternative schedule such as four days at ten hours a day or the swing shift (4pm-12am)?

Share Your Vision with Others

Now that you have created this fantastic vision for your life, your next step is to share it with others, i.e. your spouse, your team, your family, your organization, your community, and beyond. As the leader of this vision, it is important to help others understand why you're headed in a certain direction and where that direction leads. It is essential to share your vision with those who can potentially help carry it out.

Always explain why it is important, why it is worthwhile, and what kind of support you need. It is best to share your vision only after you have fully embraced the vision yourself. Get comfortable conveying and explaining the vision to others. This process involves more than including your vision statement in the signature line of your email or as a hashtag on your text messages. It requires that you write your concept on paper, answer questions in advance and rehearse in front of a mirror. By doing so, you will gain the confidence and fluidity needed to present your vision via YouTube videos, Periscope, Face Book Live and other visual media. Prepare a thirty second elevator pitch and a fifteen minutes of fame presentation so that you are always prepared to share your vision in any environment. .

Talk about your vision openly and tell stories to highlight scenarios that will help others to see the direction of your vision. Show that you care about your vision and help others to see the impact achieving your vision will make. Develop a storyboard or a visual presentation to convey the overall vision you would like to achieve. Initially your supporters may not fully agree with or embrace your vision right away, but if you share your vision frequently, confidently, and passionately, you have a much greater chance of inspiring "buy in" from others. This will encourage support as you bring your vision to life.

30-Day Challenges – Create a Vision for your Life

Life happens and often times we get inundated with our daily grind—so inundated that we go for weeks, months, even years without dreaming BIG. There are some people who don't dream at all. Take a break from your day-to-day activities and find time to dream again. The thirty day challenges below will help you get started.

30-Day Create a Vision Board and Action Plan

- Spend a day or a weekend on Pinterest and other sites planning your vision board.
- Gather your ideas and create a vision board.
- Spend no less than thirty minutes each time you work on your board throughout over the next thirty days.
- Share your vision board with at least one important person in your life on the thirtieth day.

30-Day Dream BIG Challenge

- On the first day, write down one dream that you have and would like to pursue.
- Day two—add something additional to your dream. For example, if you dream of buying a five bedroom, five bath home on day one, then add a swimming pool and a gardener on day two. On day three, make it a beach house at your favorite vacation spot. Day four, make the dream bigger. You can make it as lavish or exciting or imaginative as you want.
- By day thirty, go back and read what you added each day to your original dream. See how much you allowed your mind to stretch beyond your original dream.
- If the dream was too small, repeat the process.

CHAPTER 11

Adapt and Overcome

adies, we are getting closer! The end of the book is near, but I couldn't finish without tackling one of the most arduous missions you will encounter on your journey to becoming Fit, Fabulous and Focused—specifically, to Adapt and Overcome. There will be at least one challenge, one hurdle, one disappointment, and/ or one unexpected event in your life that you must adapt to and overcome. This simple, yet life-altering, phrase may become applicable to several moments in your life. These moments will either make you or break you. You will be tested in ways you've never imagined. Adapting and overcoming will test your faith, patience, fortitude, and your resolve.

It is through adapting and overcoming the personal experiences in your life that you will find out what you are really made of. It would only be too easy if creating the life you wanted was simply a matter of creating a vision statement and executing it. If it was that easy, we would all have the life we wanted. But the reality is, we all face obstacles, challenges and hurdles. When you find yourself facing one of these moments, you will have to ask yourself, "How bad do I want to achieve my goal?" and "Is accomplishing the goal really worth the struggle?" Only you can answer these questions.

When I transitioned from the US Army to the private sector, I decided to change career fields. In the middle of my second enlistment, I decided that military life was no longer for me. I I left the field of technology in the US Army and entered the field of accounting as a civilian. I had obtained my bachelor's degree in accounting but had no experience, with the exception of volunteering as a tax preparer for soldiers during tax season. To ensure a successful and complete transition to my new civilian life, I completely severed my ties with the military. I declined to do a second tour in Europe and being planning for my transition as an accountant in the city of Atlanta. I knew it would be difficult to change career fields, but I felt it was better to make the transition early in my career instead of waiting until there was much more at stake.

So I proceeded, full speed ahead, to the next step with only my dream and my determination to keep me going. I remember receiving my first job offer from a small CPA firm for a bookkeeping position paying $8/hr. I was totally blown away. Eight bucks an hour, are you *serious?* Surely, I would get a better offer, so I waited...and waited...and waited. To my dismay, the first offer was the only one. Although I applied to several other positions, I didn't have the experience to warrant a better offer. So I had no other choice but to take the position, as I was already using my final days of military leave. Once I accepted the offer, my income and my lifestyle changed significantly overnight. I had to instantly adapt to living on $8.00/hour without benefits and without the safety net that my former military career so graciously provided. I wasn't a retiree, so there was no additional income coming in. My only remaining military benefits were the VA Hospital and burial benefits and, I didn't want to use either of those under any circumstance!

I knew I had to overcome the fear and stress of starting over to build a new career, and I had to do it quickly. I envisioned myself many times as a successful accountant in a corner office with glass windows and a beautiful view overlooking downtown Atlanta. However, the reality was that until I gained some much needed experience, all I had was my dream and my determination. But that didn't stop me. I woke up every day with a new resolve and more determined than ever. I learned everything I could in that bookkeeping position and used that experience to move on to a better position. I continued this trend for a couple of years.

But I couldn't continue changing jobs every two to three years, so once again, I had to adapt. I eventually started working for a temporary agency so that I could accept contract positions in different areas of accounting without showing an unstable job history on my resume. This calculated move allowed me to gain valuable experience in payroll, taxes, auditing, collections and bookkeeping while working for one company. Once I gained this broad base of experience, I was able to obtain a higher paying permanent position. And yes, I eventually got my corner office in downtown

Atlanta on Marietta Street as a Junior Accountant. It wasn't the view I had envisioned (I was only on the third floor) but nonetheless, I achieved my goal.

It was a rough journey to get that corner office. I had to adapt a new approach to gain experience and overcome several roadblocks that came my way. Believe me, while working in the city of Atlanta for $8.00 an hour there were plenty of obstacles! Missed car payments, no eating out, and no hanging with friends were sacrifices I simply had to make. I could only afford the essentials and barely made enough money to cover my bills and take care of my daughter. So she remained an hour away in Macon with my parents as I continued to build my career. For a few months along the way I had to rely heavily on my family as I worked to gain experience and obtain an even better position and income. But after achieving my goal of getting a corner office, I knew I could accomplish anything as long as I was willing to adapt and overcome! My journey was a stressful at times, but the outcome was definitely worth the struggle.

Beyond Your Control

I like this quote by Brian Tracy: *You cannot control what happens to you, but you can control your attitude toward what happens to you, and in that, you will be mastering change rather than allowing it to master you.*

The topic "beyond your control" has probably given me more grey hairs than I care to admit. By the age of forty, you will find there are many moments that fall into the "beyond your control" category. Like me, you may already have spent more than enough time trying to change or control several of those moments, but your personal experiences eventually prove you should do otherwise. In previous chapters I spoke of changing old habits and undesirable behaviors. Adapting and overcoming is about more than changing behaviors—it's also about letting go. It's about accepting and moving beyond your desired outcome.

There will be situations in your life when you may feel that your hopes, prayers, wishes and expectations did not yield the outcome you desired. You will be disappointed. You may also feel anger, frustration, despair, hurt, and grief. But that's a part of the process and a part of life. Maybe you didn't get the promotion you were promised or the job was given to someone with less experience or because of nepotism.

Perhaps you damaged your car in an accident that wasn't your fault, or despite your best efforts you weren't able to salvage an unhealthy relationship. Maybe your child made a series of unwise decisions regardless of the advice you provided. All of these scenarios are possible and can happen more than once in your lifetime. The key to successfully getting beyond these situations lies within you and your ability to let go of things that are beyond your control.

One of the toughest aspects of dealing with things that are beyond your control will be suppressing your innate desire to keep working towards your idea of what is "right." Just because you believe something is acceptable, fair, or best in a particular situation, those parameters may never be met. You must accept things as they are and move on. I'm not asking you to forgo the power of prayer and positive thinking, for those are both powerful allies in moving beyond things you cannot control. However, you can also move beyond those circumstances by being aware of the story you tell yourself and others about them. You can limit the amount of power and control that undesirable circumstances have in your life by understanding that what you repeatedly say about those moments is equally as important as what actually happened in that moment.

The next time you encounter circumstances that are beyond your control, try using the tips below to get beyond those moments.

- Allow yourself time to process your feelings about what happened.
- Understand that some circumstances take longer than others to overcome.
- Do not make yourself responsible for someone else's actions or behavior.
- Figure out the truth, if possible, and accept it so that you can heal and move on.
- Speak of the moment as a past event. Re-enacting the moment as if it happened today will prolong your desire to change the outcome.
- Forgive yourself. Forgive the other person.
- Accept that you cannot change the ending of a circumstance that has already happened. What is done is done. So what is your new normal?

- What is your next move? Will you continue in the relationship? Will you continue to help? Will you find another job? What will you change to keep this from happening again?

It's Okay to Burn Bridges

One of my favorite movie scenes from the movie "Need for Speed" is titled "I'm back." The scene is about a young man who got the opportunity of a lifetime and decided to walk away from corporate America—naked. He undressed himself, one piece of clothing at a time while walking down the corridor past all of his colleagues. He stopped to kiss a woman he'd been admiring throughout his time at the company. When he reached the end of the corridor, he dropped his underwear to the floor and said, "Have a nice day, you miserable bastards." When he met his friends outside they asked, "Why are you naked?" He replied, "To make sure I'd never come back."

That scene never gets old! It's the best rendition of burning a bridge I've ever seen. Years ago, the general consensus was that you shouldn't burn your bridges. The sentiment became entrenched at a time when Baby Boomers were loyal to the same company for twenty and even thirty years. That was also during a time when an employee may have worked for only one or two companies, so they relied heavily on their former employer's positive reference. Well, times have changed. I don't recommend arbitrarily ending all of your relationships and partnerships abrasively. You should always strive to end them on a positive note and maintain a good rapport. However, there may come a time when ending a toxic situation or a negative relationship is inevitable and doesn't end as planned. But you will be okay. On a professional note, loyalty and job-hopping aren't viewed in the same manner as they were twenty years ago.

In personal relationships, you will find that moving on can equate to moving up. Burning a bridge or letting go can be totally liberating. You may find that you are better off without that person or situation in your life. Salvaging the relationship may not be in your best interest. There's no value in playing small or living miserably to avoid burning bridges with an acquaintance, especially if the relationship has taken a toll on your health and well-being. Don't delay moving on. Don't wait to find a more acceptable way of letting go. Just do it. Whenever you find yourself contemplating if you should or should not burn a bridge, always ask, "Is this relationship worth salvaging?"

and "Do I really want or need to come back to this stage in my life?" and "Does this work for me?"

If your answer NO to any of these question, then it's time to move on. Try to find a way to amicably move on and move forward. But if all else fails, put on your sexiest pair of shades, collect your belongings and your emotions, and focus on being Fit, Fabulous and Focused.

Learn to Improvise

As you go about the business of becoming Fit, Fabulous and Focused, you will make a few mistakes along the way. You will miss deadlines, lose focus, and you will probably fail at something more than once. That's okay. It happens to the best of us. As these unexpected hiccups happen and frustrate you beyond your current comprehension level...don't give up. More than likely, these mishaps and missteps are simply life's way of pushing you to retool your mind, compelling you to change the way you think when you encounter challenging situations. You will be forced to improvise as you adapt and overcome.

Improvising—the art of figuring it out as you go—is your own personal secret weapon in any situation, particularly those situations in which you must adapt and overcome. It's a unique skill that is not practiced by everyone because it requires you to act spontaneously, take risks, be creative and trust yourself. Learning to improvise is like having a unique benefit and social skill that can yield amazing results if it used wisely. You may be wondering *If this skill is so beneficial, why doesn't everyone use it?* One answer is because some people are not comfortable making decisions without a plan or knowing exactly what the outcome will be. Another reason is that being creative and spontaneous doesn't come easy for some and requires lots of practice. Truthfully, the ability to adapt and overcome can often times be less difficult if you learn to improvise.

So how does this skill become tangible and when do you use it? That is totally up to you. Whether you improvise to make or produce something from whatever is available (like the actor in the television series McGyver), or you are inspired to improvise creatively like Mozart or Prince, the moment can lead you to greatness. Improvisation happens when you allow yourself to think on your feet and react in the moment without fear of the outcome.

Suck it Up, Buttercup

Unappreciated, undervalued, underestimated, underpaid, unacknowledged, unrewarded, unloved, overwhelmed, overworked, overlooked, etc. At some point in your journey to becoming Fit, Fabulous and Focused, you have more than likely experienced one or more of these feelings along the way, especially if you are a parent. Depending on how well you manage your emotions, you may tend to feel this way often. What I discovered in my late thirties was that these particular emotions come with a lot of baggage and can easily morph into self-defeating behaviors. The more pity parties and bitchfests you host will only increase your chances of experiencing these emotions on a regular basis. So what should you do when you're feeling one or all of these emotions? You suck it up, buttercup, and keep it moving!

Honestly, as a young grandmother I felt unappreciated and overwhelmed for so long, I literally thought that God was angry with me. I remember crying myself to sleep longing to comprehend why I was chosen to take on such a gargantuan role at such a young age. I was the youngest of my siblings. I had two older sisters who were much more established in their lives than I was, and my mother had passed away years ago. After a while, it seemed like every problem I solved, every crisis I endured, and every emergency I managed to avoid in my new role as Mimi came without a simple thank you or a job well done. There was no one to say, "I appreciate your help," or to give me a pat on the back. And the issues seemed to keep coming, day after day. I woke up complaining and I went to bed complaining and nothing changed. It became my way of life. It felt like no one heard me, and no one cared enough to fix my life.

Eventually I realized that my life was not going to get fixed. There was nothing wrong it and nothing wrong with me. I was a grandmother in my thirties. That was my new normal. It wasn't how I imagined it to be and it was a hell of a lot harder than I wanted it to be, but ultimately I got tired of complaining and tired of being miserable. I decided it was time to evolve. No more pity parties, no more temper tantrums, no more angry prayers. I had to toughen up and shake loose from those feelings. I had to suck it up, embrace my new role, and move on.

Don't let anyone tell you different. It takes courage to suck it up and move beyond a difficult point in your life. It doesn't happen overnight. It takes commitment to adapt and realign in a totally new direction, especially if it was by design and not by choice. I've watched women struggle with the normalcy of being single long after the divorce papers are signed. I see women adjust to becoming mothers and stepmothers the second time around. I have colleagues who struggle with unplanned career changes and financial setbacks, but they made it happen. As you find yourself handling situations by wallowing in self-pity or waiting for a different outcome, you will have to learn to suck it up, buttercup. Take setbacks in stride and if possible, make plans to prevent the same types of unwanted occurrences from happening in the future. Learn from your mistakes and march forward.

If you find yourself stuck in your feelings and have trouble learning to suck it up, try a few or all of the tips below.

- Acknowledge what is happening in your life. Don't lie to yourself (keep it real).
- Accept your new normal. Embrace it. It may only be temporary, but you will struggle as long as you deny it.
- Pat yourself on the back. Stop waiting for others to validate your efforts.
- Listen to yourself complain. Record it and play it back. You will grow tired of hearing it.
- Let go of the notion that life should be fair. Life has never, ever been fair. You will lose valuable chunks of time if you are waiting for the "fairness fairy" to materialize. Hint: she won't.

Survival Mode

When facing tough situations and hardships, you may find yourself operating in survival mode. This mode is when you unconsciously slip into doing just enough to keep your head above water. During each crisis you will likely become mentally, physically, and/or emotionally drained from battling overwhelming circumstances—circumstances that are often beyond your control. By not accepting that those circumstances are beyond your control, you internalize future situations fearfully or see them as potential failures. This makes it difficult for you to adapt and overcome during the next situation.

Survival mode feels like your back is against the wall and your options are limited. I know. I operated in survival mode many times during my thirties. You want so desperately to change an outcome or simply make a situation go away, but that is not an option. Eventually you find yourself overcome by stress and anxiety to the point that you operate on auto-pilot. You merely exist and function without truly engaging emotionally in situations. You protect your feelings at all cost and deal with your emotions only if you have to. You find other things such as part-time jobs, the kids, or longer hours at work to keep you distracted and your mind occupied. My distraction was writing at the bookstore. To avoid engaging my feelings and dealing with things that were beyond my control, I sat at the bookstore every night until it closed before driving home slowly and reentering my life.

As I mentioned earlier, this mode is often unconscious. In order to get beyond survival mode, we have to consciously engage in those emotions and situations that cause us the most angst. That's how we learn to adapt and overcome as these moments occur instead of dealing with them years later when it's much harder. It's not an easy task, and the more frequently you allow yourself to function in survival mode, the harder it will be to wean yourself from this mindset.

My suggestion is to start slowly. Avoiding survival mode takes time. I handle situations differently now than in my thirties, because I'm equipped to do so. It wasn't just a matter of turning forty, it was also an understanding there will be things that happen that are beyond my control. I stopped stressing about preventing those situations from happening and learned to prepare for them as they occurred. I learned how not to allow my intuition be overshadowed by my fear. Although they both stem from emotions, my intuition often brought on a sense of calmness and confidence, while my fear left me feeling helpless and panicked.

Finally, I upgraded my perspective. I wrote a list of my goals and prioritized them. I began working on them one by one and slowly gained the desire to reengage in my emotions and became excited about new projects and new endeavors, and less focused on the outcomes. It took a few years, but I no longer operate in survival mode. I know that hardships and difficulties will happen, and now deal with them in real time—not after the fact. I know that come what may, "This too shall pass."

CHAPTER 12

Assemble Your Dream Team

t's crunch time, ladies! Now close your eyes and take a deep breath. You're in the final phase of becoming Fit, Fabulous and Focused! Now that you've developed an award-winning vision for your life, you will need to assemble your dream to help you carry that vision onward. Your need the right team of supporters, mentors, coaches, accountability partners, advisors and cheerleaders to maximize your potential! It's time to surround yourself with people who can and will help you achieve your goals. Women have the tendency to look inward for assistance and support. We immediately think of our close friends and family members when we assemble our teams. That's a good place to start. As you transition your life to becoming Fit, Fabulous and Focused, you must expand your inner circle to include others outside of family who will motivate, cultivate, and inspire you to be great—or to be better than great...to be Fabulous!

Assembling a dream team takes a bit of strategy and planning. Years ago when I fell in love with pole dancing, I knew after attending a few more classes that I wanted to own a similar business. It was an extraordinary to experience the invigoration of working out with other women, and I wanted create that same "esprit de corps"—the pride, fellowship, and loyalty— in a studio of my own. I didn't have the experience to open a business, but I had a burning desire! So I began telling others about my dream business. I knew I couldn't do this alone and was very fortunate to have friends, family and colleagues who were willing to contribute monetarily and emotionally. I extended my partnerships to include a mentor at a non-profit business development center who helped me develop my business plan, a local web designer who taught me how to expand my brand, and other entrepreneurs who shared numerous tips on how to open and stay in business.

My dream team didn't consist of people with prestigious titles or executive positions, and yours doesn't have to either. A lofty title doesn't automatically mean someone is willing to generously share their knowledge and expertise. As you assemble your dream team, try partnering with successful entrepreneurs and others who are in the position you aspire to hold. Seek out individuals who have extensive knowledge or experience in the same industry in which you want to succeed. Ask for referrals to find a great banking partner or financial planner as you take control of your finances. Visit a local gym or team up with a committed co-worker to keep you motivated and focused on your fitness goals. Start a meet-up group to assemble your peers in the community who share similar interest and common goals. Purchase books written by others with similar visions who've experienced success in bringing theirs to life.

Evaluate Your Current Team

In his book "Think like a Success, Act like a Success," Steve Harvey's analogy about evaluating your team and the people in your life is one of the best I've heard thus far. To paraphrase, he advises that we make a list of the people who are on our team and assess the roles they play in our lives. After assessing their roles, he advises that we remove people who are not positive contributors to our vision. That's great advice.

Now that you are setting the goals required to achieve your vision, have you given any thought to the people that surround you? When is the last time you assessed your inner circle? Steve also mentions, "Sometimes your team decreases in size, but it increases in value. As you build your dream team, know that is okay if you can't bring everyone along with you on your journey."

I wholeheartedly agree with Steve Harvey. As you pursue your quest to become Fit, Fabulous and Focused, you will find it difficult to reach your goals if you are carrying someone else's debt, issues, stress or negativity along the way. You need to remove them from your team. You are not responsible for their success or their happiness; however you are responsible for your own. If you constantly experience setbacks, hurdles and missteps because of an individual contributor in your current inner circle, it's time to allow them to move on to be a contributor to someone else's team.

When assessing the members of you team, ask yourself the following:

- Do they add value to the team?
- If so, how do they contribute to your team's success?
- Do they provide positive influence and maintain a positive attitude?
- Do they have integrity? Are they trustworthy?
- Are they emotionally mature?
- Do their talents compliment the team?
- Do they have your best interests in mind? At heart?
- Are they honest, and do they want the best for you? Do they "keep it real?"

Reassemble, downsize or get a completely new team if needed. If you are currently the smartest person on your team, then you need a new team! Include people who understand that changes will happen and trust your judgment to do what is necessary to continue moving forward.

Set Clear Expectations

You are the originator of a dream, vision and plan. As you kick start the mission and step out on faith to lead your dream team to success, make sure that you have clearly defined your vision and your goals to your team. Set up one-on-one meetings to discuss expectations. Explain why you are assembling a team in the first place. Give them a reason to get excited and motivated to take this journey with you. Give them a reason to believe in you and what you intend to do. Once you do this, then you can set clear expectations and build trust within your team. As you set expectations, always keep in mind the following simple rules:

People can't read minds, and neither can you. Ensure that you include all of necessary details to successfully meet your expectations. Using S.M.A.R.T. goals can help you achieve this (more about that in Chapter 14).

Don't assume because you say it, so shall it be done. You are not a dictator and this is not the military. Make sure that you have mutual consent from individual team members once you have set your expectations.

Hold your team accountable to the expectations. Once the expectations are clearly stated and you have mutual consent, then make sure everyone pulls their weight. If they are not capable or unwilling to meet expectations, be prepared to release them from their role and the team if needed.

Define roles for each team member. Identify what positions each team members should have. What is the best fit for your current team as they work side-by-side to carry out your vision? Personal assistant, hair stylist, nanny, fill-in babysitter, financial planner, banker, tax preparer, prayer partners, exercise partner, etc.—all fill a crucial role. Identifying roles according to your specific needs and then matching people with those roles will add clarity and transparency to your intentions.

Repurpose Your Team (if Needed)

Be flexible and nimble enough to adjust your team as changes happen. This is a key component in sustaining a successful team and achieving your vision. I'm not suggesting that you should rewrite your vision and throw out your goals with every change in your career field or industry. However, you should make adjustments with your team, if needed, when growth happens.

If your industry or profession has changed significantly over the years, you should extend the resources to stay abreast of those changes and share them with your team. For instance, if you own a hair salon, then encourage your team to attend hair shows to learn new color or hair weave techniques to stay current and relevant with market demands. If you are you are a chef, update your menu and try adding gluten free meals or weekly meal plans to attract new customers. If you are a personal trainer, work with your team's web designer to develop a series of 10-minute on-the-go video clips for clients with busy schedules to encourage fitness throughout the day. If you lack knowledge at work on your 9-to-5, don't be afraid to ask for cross training or a stretch assignment on your job to ensure growth and development for you and your team.

Several huge corporations of the past suffered tremendous setbacks and lost their industry advantage because they refused to repurpose their teams. They ignored market demands in favor of the status quo. Blockbuster, Eastman Kodak, Motorola, US Postal Service, Blackberry, Hummer, and JC Penney are just a few of the most familiar, huge entities who failed to be flexible and nimble enough to change with the times. Now they are no longer giants of their industry. The same failures can happen on a much smaller level if you are unwilling to repurpose your team.

Create New Opportunities

Last but certainly not least, you want to keep your team engaged and excited by creating new opportunities. Ask for their input often and try incorporating their feedback as you launch new programs or new initiatives. If your goal is to increase your website traffic by 25%, your team might recommend increasing your presence on social media to get additional exposure while cross posting links to your website. Once you identify this new opportunity, strategize with your team to develop a plan to launch a Twitter, Facebook, Instagram account and Pinterest. As you assemble your dream team, it is essential to motivate them, inspire them, encourage them, and thank them. But most importantly it's imperative to listen to them as well.

Maybe you've decided to expand your brand. Be innovative and inspire your team to work together on projects and solve problems. Don't force the opportunity. Make it as organic as possible. Great ideas and innovation take time. Allow your team the time it takes to cohesively work together while you plan ahead and forward think about the next new initiative.

Ensure that you provide your team with the tools they need to be successful as they seize this new opportunity, such as a centralized location with parking, Wi-Fi access, supplies, even coffee, cream and sugar for early morning or late night meetings. Encourage team members to generate new ideas and then recognize their efforts. Praise and kudos go a long way in motivating your team to do their best. Get together once a quarter and do something interesting and unexpected to spark a few new ideas.

30-Day Challenges —Assemble Your Dream Team

Nurture your team and help your team members shine! The challenges below can help you be the leader your team needs and deserves.

30-Day Challenge: Organize your Team Base

- Clear out old emails. If you need them for future reference, store them on the cloud or on an external drive for safe keeping.
- Get rid of old contacts from your phone.
- Delete old text messages from your mobile devices.
- Encourage your team to do the same so they can become organized and efficient.

30-Day Challenge: Find a Mentor

- Google the Chamber of Commerce and local business clubs to identify movers and shakers within your community.
- Don't overlook the wise old souls who know a lot about human relations and real world experiences. Research retired professors, business leaders and society mavens who know what it takes to become successful.
- Reach out—don't be shy! Chances are, someone will feel honored to become your mentor.

30-Day Challenge: Connect Outside of Social Media

- Go where the action is. Attend meetings and networking groups. Seek out social activities that require face-to-face interaction.
- Join a walking group, a breakfast club, or a class at church.
- Consider a speed dating adventure and get to know a multitude of people in mere seconds!
- Strike up conversations at the bookstore, the local coffee shop, the gym or the park.
- Become empowered through conversation and friendly discourse.

30-Day Challenge: Start a Meet Up Group in Your City

- Join a meet-up group by and for aficionados in your same field. Soak up their wisdom while socializing.
- Better yet, start your own group and attract like-minded people who enjoy sharing their own dreams, visions and goals.
- If you have more than one passion, join or start several meet-up groups and revel in the authenticity of personal connections.

CHAPTER 13

Ask for What You Really Want and Be Specific

Over the years, I've had many in-depth conversations with women about what they want in life. More often than not, the conversations started with a generic list of wants such as:

- Supportive partner
- Good marriage
- Healthy children
- Financial freedom
- Personal happiness
- Good health

But after spending hours chatting about needs, desires, hopes and dreams, the conversation would unconsciously shift from what they do want to what they don't want. Thus, we would only have a vague and ambiguous list of answers that provide very little insight to the question at hand: *"What do I really want?"* You see, the generic big picture answers given by women are not due to an absence of understanding or intentional avoidance. The generalities arise because many women simply don't know what they want "specifically."

Society, the media, parents, pastors and other influential figures train women from young childhood to be nonaggressive and polite. To be direct about our personal desires in life has been, until very recently, discouraged. An unwritten rule among women is that if we put our wants above our family's wants, we are negligent. Likewise, if we put our needs above the needs of our significant other in a relationship, we are selfish. There is little or no balance in these matters, meaning women often live an unbalanced life.

Develop Your Own Happiness Equation

Ladies, you hold the keys to a "Happiness Equation." It is yours to develop, once you get past some age-old stumbling blocks. For instance, when it comes to being specific about pursuing our dreams, we are often afraid of what others will think or afraid of having our ideas rejected by loved ones. We avoid being "judged" for behaving, acting or even feeling in ways that are anathema to our upbringing. Women have selflessly operated under a weight of expectations for centuries, although these expectations largely benefit others and not ourselves. So we "play by the rules" and suppress our desires. We humbly accept what is offered and do our duty.

Professionally, some women cling to the notion that their boss will recognize their hard work and unwavering efforts, and believe they will be rewarded because it's the right thing to do. Women often sabotage their own careers by not speaking confidently and positively about their own achievements and desire to get ahead. During annual reviews and contract negotiations, we fail to ask for what we want and succumb to our fears, leaving the negotiation table feeling less than worthy, short changed, or disappointed.

The joy of being Fit, Fabulous and Focused is that we become empowered to find a better balance at work, at home, and in our relationships. We learn to include ourselves in our own personal "Happiness Equation"—an equation that is ours to customize and develop individually. We can become authors our own "happiness equation." It begins by asking ourselves what we really want, and I mean "specifically." It requires that we define what matters, in detail. So how do you ask for what you really want "specifically," and how do you define what matters? You can start with the following checklist.

Making a List and Checking it Twice

- Create a list of the things you want
- Create a list of things that make you happy
- Merge both lists
- Prioritize items on each list
- Make a plan that incorporates your wants and the things that make you happy
- Practice asking for what you want
- Make the effort to participate in what makes you happy
- Prepare to get what you want…and reap the happiness of a well thought out plan.

There are other factors involved in this process, but let's first explore the concepts above to gain a greater understanding how to put words into action.

1. Create a List

If you are going to create the life you want after forty, first you must figure out what you want in your life. You can start by making a list and checking it twice. This list can be about your professional endeavors or your personal goals. Be sure to include travel, family and wellness goals. Create your list without considering your current financial state. Adding financial pressure to the equation may keep you from thinking with an open mind.

As you identify what you want and create your list, don't hold back. No matter how bold or unattainable you think your ideas may be, write them anyway. If you experience difficulty in making your list, try thinking of what you loved to do before you started your current career. Think of things you loved to do as a child or that you planned to do after you completed high school or college. What about the ideas you exchanged with your bestie while hanging out after church, or the dreams you put on hold in your thirties?

Allow yourself plenty of time to think as you jot down your list. Be specific. This will clarity to your list of wants, and will also help with decision making and prioritizing your future endeavors. Establish measurable timelines for projects and goals.

Minimize ambiguity by excluding phrases like "real soon" and "in the future" and "more often." Those words are open ended and always left to interpretation. Set clear, concrete expectations for what you want and need up front. This will allow others to communicate that they are willing and able to meet your expectations, or not. Lastly, once you review your list of wants, then you can determine if your list is realistic and what it will take to achieve it.

2. Prioritize Your List (Top Five)

After you've made a list of what you want, prioritize your list. Circle or highlight the top five things most important things on your list. Whether it's your relationship, your career, your family, or your education, or your own business, identify what makes you happy, what motivates you, what you're passionate about, what you are willing to tolerate, and what is an absolute must have in your life. You can only have five goals in this exercise, so it may take some time to figure out what matters most. If you are having trouble prioritizing, try asking yourself if the item on your list is an option or an obligation? Ask yourself if the item on your list is important, or is it urgent?

According to Warren Buffett, once you've identified your top five goals, put the remaining goals on a separate list and title it your "Avoid at all cost" list. Buffet explains that once you've identified your top five, the remaining items on your "Avoid at all cost" list get no attention until you've successfully completed your top five.

3. Make a Plan

Now comes the details—the action plan. How do you intend to accomplish the goals on your list? What steps have you taken to get started? What are your current resources and support systems? Are they adequate enough to support your goals? Do you need to brush up on your techniques or acquire additional education? Do you have the skill set required to accomplish your top five? If not, are you going back to school or attending seminars? Do you need to relocate to accomplish your goals? How about your resume or your curriculum vitae, are they up to par? Do you have a mentor or peer group support as you work on your goals?

Ladies you can write a thousand lists and prioritize them all day, but without a plan of action to accomplish your goals, your list are merely words written on a piece of paper. After all, we are doing important and life changing work throughout this exercise, and it takes effort. We are seeking to balance life's demands with our own goals so that we can author our own "Happiness Equation." It is imperative that we answer the questions above before tackling our top five. Hint: this process will save you a lot of stress and minimize a few obstacles along the way. Once you identify what you need to accomplish your goals, you can make it known and ask for support as needed. An easy way to set up your plan for your top five goals is to create a template like the one below.

When I decided to make an action plan for my top five, I listed my goals, how to accomplish my goals and the desired results for each goal in a template. By visually posting my plan, it felt tangible and concrete. I could attach it to my mirror, my vision board or to my whiteboard at the office. I made sure that each goal had a measurable time line associated with it. Goals and timelines are not mutually exclusive and should be treated as one. Viewing them as separate items encourages procrastination and a lack of focus. It also removes the accountability needed to execute your plan.

FUTURE GOAL	HOW TO ACCOMPLISH	DESIRED RESULT

4. Practice Asking For What You Want

Ever heard of the saying "Practice makes perfect?" Well, it does indeed. Asking for what you may not come easy or naturally for every woman, so the best way to become proficient and get comfortable is to practice. You can start small and practice in the mirror alone. As you build your confidence level, ask your partner or your bestie to give you candid feedback on your technique. Or you can take a giant leap of faith and decide that it doesn't matter which approach you take, as long as you practice. Soon you'll be asking for what you want, and that is a major step forward!

When communicating what you want to others, ensure that you're specific about what you want and when you want it. This is especially important if you are communicating to more than one person. Find ways to make your request a win/win situation for all parties involved. If you are asking for a promotion by the end of the year, identify what your company can expect from your level of performance in exchange for that promotion. If you are raising your rates for the services you provide to customers, create a brochure or video clip highlighting the "value added" services you offer in exchange for the higher rates.

But don't simply practice asking for what you want and getting a favorable response; prepare yourself for different responses to your request. Prepare to be challenged. Practice hearing outcomes that may differ from your expectations, such as "We are not quite sure that you are ready for a promotion to management at this time, but perhaps we can meet again in the future," or "Although you have an impressive credit score and an extensive business plan, we've made a decision to decline your request for a small business loan at this time." Role-play different scenarios that require you to be direct and assertive as you convey your desires to others, or rehearse moments that require you to maintain your composure if you feel emotional while asking for what you want. You can even coach yourself on not taking it personally or overreacting if negotiations don't go as planned.

If negotiating is a part of the process, remember to maintain a balance of respect and persistence. Be prepared that you may not get what you want right away. This should not deter you from regrouping and asking again with a different approach. Stay positive and determined. If you weren't effective the first time around, prepare for the second time around. As you train to perfect your technique, pause and take a moment to review your approach and tweak it as necessary. Every situation is different and what worked for one scenario may not work well for another. Practice, practice, practice!

5. Be Prepared To Get What You Ask For

After getting promotions and climbing the corporate ladder, I can't tell you the number of times I thought to myself, *Damn, do I really want this? Do I really want to work those long hours and sit in meetings all the time? Do I really want to work through lunch and take work home after a long day at the office?* When I bought my house at the age of thirty, I remember sobbing silently in my car when I struggled to pay for basic home repairs that I couldn't afford. Did I truly want to deal with the maintenance cost of owning a home? At 30 years old, did I even understand what those costs were? I wish I had known more about home maintenance cost before taking the plunge and buying a home. I did tons of research on how to acquire my house and improve my credit score, but I never fathomed the amount of money it would take to maintain a historic home.

Do you want a bigger house or a promotion on your job? Are you combing the aisles at the dealership in search of your dream car? Are you asking for startup capital for your new business idea or seeking Angel investors to help you grow your current small business? Maybe you would like more free time to travel and see the world, or perhaps you want a bigger family? Is your goal to finish your degree? Maybe you wanted to become a best-selling author and sell thousands of books. I could go on and on, but the real question is "Are you prepared to get it?"

Are you ready to handle what comes along with creating the life you want? Are you ready to sacrifice time away from your family for prolonged periods as you work long hours for that promotion? Can you afford the exorbitant maintenance costs and the premium gas it takes to keep your new BMW 750 running smoothly? Are you prepared to exchange a percentage of your business for a much needed investment from an Angel investor? These questions are not meant to deter you or discourage you. They are meant to ensure that you've given some thought to getting what you're asking for.

Being prepared to get what you want will not only minimize the stress, but it will also help you stick to your plan when times get tough. If you've done an ample amount of preparation, you are more likely to hang in there when things don't go exactly as planned.

Take Risks

There's no exact science to taking risks. Each new risk you encounter is as unpredictable and potentially overwhelming as the last. Depending on where you are in your journey to create the life you want, there are hundreds of mottos and mantras to adopt about risk taking. These uplifting and challenging words can help keep you focused and motivated. You might indulge in self-help books like this one, or attend webinars on risk taking before you actually take that first step. All the power quotes you've heard in the past, like "Think outside the box," and "Get out of your comfort zone," and "Get out of your own way," and "Step out on faith," are all applicable when taking risks. As you encounter risk, don't sabotage your efforts by contemplating "what ifs." If you have a strong aversion to taking risks, try asking yourself the questions below.

What if something goes wrong?

It probably will, but not to the level your overactive imagination might conjure. If you planned and prepared for your success, you will be able to get back on track. Just think "What if something goes right!"

What if I can't handle the risk?

Stop doubting yourself and don't underestimate your ability to handle the consequences of risk. As the consequences arise, pause to assess the risk and revise your plan as needed. If I had succumbed to the numerous moments of self-doubt I encountered while writing my business plan for my pole-fitness studio, I would never have opened at all. If necessary, don't be afraid to scrap your original plan and start again.

Should I play it safe and wait for a better opportunity?

The truth is that every deal is not a good deal, and every offer is not for you. However, the "perfect offer" may be a figment of your imagination. Are you really waiting for a better opportunity or are you simply making excuses because you are afraid to take risks? Playing it safe doesn't mean things will eventually get better or that a better offer will come along. Settling for the status quo may not be feasible or in your best interest, especially if your current situation isn't working well for you right now.

What if I fail?

Setbacks, hurdles, obstacles, stumbles, missteps, hardships, and failures will happen in some form or another throughout your journey to create the life you want. It's inevitable, and it's okay! You may even encounter failure more than once, but don't give up. I think Oprah said it best at her Harvard Commencement speech in 2016. "There is no such thing as failure. Failure is just life trying to move us in another direction."

Know Your Worth

Years ago in my twenties I was hanging with a guy who I considered to be a very good friend. We were exchanging stories about our future goals and expectations of our potential mates. As the conversation continued, he turned to me and said, "You know what, I think maybe you expect a little bit more than is warranted." I remember thinking to myself, *Wow, is this because I said I deserved to date a man who doesn't smoke weed and had a career?* Knowing your worth goes well beyond dollars and cents. This is not only applicable to women in business, it's applicable to your personal life, as well. Knowing your worth is a culmination of your self-esteem, self-respect, and self-confidence all rolled into one. All of these elements are integral and fundamental to determining your worth. Without one of these key elements in place, you can almost guarantee that you will undermine, under value, or under appreciate your worth either personally or professionally.

Likewise, know your strengths and know what you bring to the table. Whether you are seeking a soul mate or changing careers, this information is just good to know. You have to take stock of your tangible assets, as well as your intangible assets. There will always be someone who can do what you do faster, smarter and better, but that should have no impact on how you determine what you are worth. Comparing yourself to others and measuring your accomplishments or lifestyle against your peers is a sure fire way to develop self-defeating behaviors that can take years to overcome.

Don't seek the validation or approval of others. Seeking validation is equally as detrimental to your self-esteem as comparing yourself to others. You must learn to think highly of yourself and your decisions regardless of the opinions of others. Accept that you cannot control what others think. Taking a leap of faith might seem much easier if only you could get the approval of friends, colleagues or family members, but you must stay focused and determined even in the absence of their approval.

As you shift your outlook to acknowledge your worth, you may encounter those who doubt, question, and criticize your assessment of your worth. Ignore the rhetoric and move forward with your plan. As a business owner, you can acknowledge your worth by finding a way to add value to your products and services. Reevaluate your pricing structure so that you can confidently charge more for the services you provide. As an employee, reassess your current level of expertise and sharpen your negotiating skills so that you are prepared to ask for that raise at work. In your personal life, raise your level of expectation for yourself, your friends and your loved ones. Be willing to end those relationships that are toxic and unfavorable in your pursuit of becoming Fit, Fabulous and Focused.

Learn to Negotiate

I will be the first to admit that negotiating is not my forte, at least not yet. I have struggled mightily with the art of negotiation throughout my career and in my personal life, mainly because I didn't know my worth. Years ago as I progressed in my career in the private sector, I was exposed to salary negotiations to some extent. After becoming an employee of the municipal government, salary negotiations were non-existent. As a business owner, I learned too little, too late about setting prices and negotiating better rates with my customers. By my fifth year in business, I had burned through all of my working capital. Although I loved my pole fitness business and clientele, I was mentally exhausted from working harder rather than smarter.

Learning to negotiate is a skill that should not be discounted or minimized. Negotiating involves more than beating your opponent and winning arguments. Skillful negotiating requires preparation, strategizing, listening, being open to creative thinking, and partnering to get the desired outcome for all parties involved. It is a skill that should be used in your personal and professional life often. As you pursue your goal of becoming Fit, Fabulous and Focused, I recommend that you invest in an audio book such as "The Negotiator in You" by Joshua N. Weiss, Ph.D. Once you expand your knowledge of negotiating techniques, take advantage of opportunities that allow you to implement and practice what you've learned.

Don't Apologize

My final tip in asking for what you want is "Don't apologize for asking." It is up to you to determine your worth and pursue what you feel you deserve in life. Pursue it passionately and vehemently without regret or guilt. It is time to stop explaining your worth to others and time to start confidently communicating the value of who you are.

When you know what YOU know, why entertain what THEY think?

30-Day Challenges —Ask for What You Want

Build courage and confidence by asking for what you want. The 30-Day challenges below can help you ask for what you really want in specific terms.

30-Day Challenge: Become a Better Speaker

- Try not to use "uh" or "mmm" while speaking publicly.
- If you are speaking to an audience and feel an "uh" or "mmm" coming on, take a breather. Pause or slow down and take a moment to collect your thoughts.
- Practice speaking publicly before an event. Practice makes perfect.

30-Day Challenge: The Discount Challenge

- Choose a restaurant or retailer and purchase an item.
- Ask for a 10% discount with no rhyme or reason.
- Repeat the process daily over the thirty day period.

30-Day Challenge: Ask for it Challenge

- Spend thirty days asking for things you want or need.
- Find something new to ask for every day
    - Help with a project/chore
    - Information
    - Perks
    - Directions
    - Feedback
    - Favors
    - Raises
    - Discounts
    - Love/Sex
    - Attention
    - More Paid Time Off
    - Quality Time
    - More Romance
    - Financial Assistance

CHAPTER 14

Start Today

Finally! We have made it to the last chapter of this wonderful guide to becoming Fit, Fabulous and Focused. I thought long and hard about this chapter and asked myself what final pearls of wisdom could be shared to impact your personal journey as you create the life you want after forty. So I titled my final chapter "START TODAY." No more making excuses, no more procrastinating, and no more being paralyzed by the fear of failing. START TODAY!

Yes! Opening a business, going back to school, accepting a promotion, moving to a new city, adopting a healthier lifestyle, losing weight, changing careers, living a debt free life, building your dream home, writing a book, quitting your job, starting a charity, taking dream vacations and becoming a millionaire are all huge endeavors. The thought of tackling one of the dreams on this list or many others you have on your list may seem overwhelming or unachievable. Luck and opportunity will not get you there. Until you transform your dreams into specific goals with measurable, achievable, time-bound steps, you will continue to only dream of the day you will get started!

We've already discussed how to create the specific action steps needed to transform your dreams into goals in the previous chapters: Creating an Action Plan, Assembling Your Dream Team and Asking for What You Want. So you know what to do, and now the only thing left is to get started!

When I began my job search to leave my previous job, I remember having a heightened feeling of anxiousness for a new start. It felt like I thought about changing my life and my surroundings every minute of the day. During my job search, I didn't apply for very many positions and had no idea that my search would lead me to a job that was 109 miles away from home. I wasn't particularly fond of the idea of moving away, but I was beyond exhausted with working for organizations with no opportunities to advance my career. I wanted so much more than my current situation could offer. I needed a fresh start, so I accepted the position! I could easily have made excuses to give up and never leave Macon. I could have accepted a position that was a lot closer to home. But my desire to grow wouldn't let me. A fresh start was what I wanted. A fresh start was what I needed. And I needed to START TODAY!!

Only you can determine when you are ready to create the life you want. All of your to-do lists, plans, dream journals and vision boards won't matter if you don't rise to the occasion and START TODAY. What are you waiting for?

One Dream at a Time

Although I now have the time and resources to properly nurture several of my dreams to fruition, I choose to focus on one dream at a time. Focusing on too many endeavors all at once can be overwhelming and highly unproductive. It can also be very distracting and expensive. Limit the number of dreams you pursue at one time. Pulling yourself in too many directions is sure fire way to get sabotage your efforts.

Prioritize your dreams according to the ones that are the most important to you. Take time to figure out what you want. Is this really your dream, or is it someone else's dream, like your spouse or your family members? Typically, I don't waste my resources chasing dreams that are on the bottom of my list (see Warren Buffet's Top 5 in Chapter 13). I treat my dreams like a series of steps, each one leading to something bigger and better.

Evaluate what tools and skills are needed to achieve your goal. If you don't have those skills can, can you easily acquire them and how long will it take? I focus my energy and efforts on chasing the dreams that compliment and support my vision.

Decide if you are ready for the level of commitment and risk required to achieve your goal. Are you ready to focus on your goal through completion no matter how long it takes? Nurturing my dreams are my number one priority. I share them, work on them, and support them daily.

Don't allow false starts or a few hurdles along the way discourage you. It is imperative that you stay focused and follow one course until you are successful. Avoid engaging in activities and other goals that are not your top priority. Say no to those impulses and distractions that appeal to you while pursuing your dream.

Work S.M.A.R.T.-er (Not Harder)

Set S.M.A.R.T. goals—meaning goals that are Specific, Measurable, Attainable, Relevant and Timely. This means your goals and objectives are concrete and can be weighed, evaluated, assessed, verified and benchmarked. In other words, your resolutions are clear, you are on course, your journey is moving forward, and you can track your progress. S.M.A.R.T. goal setting propels you onward toward achievement.

S - Specific: precise, detailed, concrete, non-vague
M - Measurable: identifiable, obvious, evidenced by progress
A - Attainable: realistic, doable, bite-sized, something you can achieve with effort
R - Relevant: a priority, what matters most, a meaningful component
T - Timely: a timeframe, a deadline, a defined space on your calendar

Remind Yourself of Why You Love It

It's easy to get side tracked and lose focus on your dreams and goals. As a working woman in today's society, multitasking is the new normal. You spend the majority of your day managing meetings, planning date nights, and being your teenager's personal Uber driver. So if you find yourself losing focus or not being in the mood to start today, try reminding yourself why you love your dream. Remind yourself why you chose this particular dream. You may be able to jumpstart your motor with minimal effort by simply listening to classical music, or your "stall" may prompt you to take a continuing education class at a local university to bolster a skill set.

If you find yourself stuck in quicksand too often, then by all means try the following:

1. Create a journal. Write down the exciting things that happen daily and week-ly as you start the process. Write down the successes and the failures as they happen. A year from now as you reflect on your journey, you can read your journal and celebrate the milestones or avoid making the same mistakes twice.

2. Adopt a mantra that motivates you and repeat it to yourself daily. Post it on your wall, on your desk at work, in your car, even as a screen saver on your phone. My current mantra is "Make today so awesome that yesterday gets jealous." Create a vision board and focus on it daily.

3. Phone a friend. If you've shared your dream with others, reach out to them and rekindle conversations about your dreams. Talk about the moments that led you to your goal. Allow your friend to reignite your passion and reinvigo-rate your drive.

It's okay to get stuck every now and then. We've all had days that challenge our thoughts, but don't allow a bad day or a rough moment to prevent you from getting started. And once you get started, don't allow a few failures to discourage you. Often failure is part of the journey and teaches us how "not" to fail again.

Dream Big and Give Yourself Something to Strive For

One of the first hurdles to tackle as you shift your mindset to becoming Fit, Fabulous and Focused is to change the way you dream. You have to dream big and give yourself something to strive for. I am guilty of having small dreams. Over the years, I allowed the pressures and distractions of my everyday life limit my dreams. My dreams matched my skill level and I became stagnant. I became so consumed that my focus was no longer on my dreams, it was on the obstacles and hurdles I experienced in my thirties. I took the following steps to remind myself to dream big.

Visualize your Success

What will you do once you achieve the dream? Yes, you must be prepared for the day when it comes to fruition. So get out your legal pad, dream journal, laptop, or your vision board (whichever you prefer) and pour a glass of your favorite cocktail and visualize your dream. Imagine what it will feel like when you pay for your children's education, purchase commercial property, earn $1 million a year, leave your job without needing another job, purchase your dream car in cash, hire a driver and a housekeeper, take extended vacations several times a year, build your dream home, fly first class, write a book, start a non-profit organization to help others.

Repeat this process often. The list below will help inspire you as you visualize all you can be.

- Learn from the past so you won't repeat it. Lessons are precious and remind us of what NOT to do!
- Remember, failure is just a new opportunity to do something differently.
- Don't drift through life, but rather lead a life of purpose. Plan so that you can fulfill your purpose.
- Be an active participant in your future. Put yourself in charge. Be a change agent. Boss up!

Plan for Success

Yes! You should plan for your success. Why? Because you need to be prepared for when it happens! It is not enough to simply plan to get started or to plan how to achieve your goals. Planning for success is essential if you want to enjoy it and reap the rewards. Think of the countless power ball lottery winners who crashed and burned. Their stories are about winning big and losing it all, dead broke or worse. Just take a look at celebrities like Mike Tyson and Lindsey Lohan who reached the height of superstardom in their A-List careers, only to find themselves out of work or out of money in only a few short years. Perhaps they didn't know how to plan for success or "deal" with success once they found it. They didn't equip themselves to attend to the details that success requires. Therefore, they had no proper plan for sustaining their success. In other words, planning is a powerful tool that helps ensure and curate success.

Your dreams and goals deserve a plan. Pay attention to your plans to that you can nurture the dream. This is a mutually assured win/win and will help catapult you to the finish line.

Allow Your Dreams to Manifest

After you create your vision, assemble your team, and specifically ask for what you want, you must prepare a solid platform from which your dreams can spring. That platform is YOU. You are the vessel through which all this will happen. Your dreams will manifest—become visible and undeniable—when they originate from a place of peace and health. The wellbeing of your mind and body is incredibly essential in your journey toward becoming Fit, Fabulous and Focused. This involves taking care of the basics of YOU. Below are a few reminders that certainly help at any age, but especially after the age of forty.

- Listen to the experts and get enough rest! Recuperative sleep allows your brain and body to rejuvenate.
- Hydrate your brain by drinking plenty of water. This helps your mind (and bodily organs) to function optimally.
- Eat foods that contribute to your health. Natural and unprocessed foods are best for your body, and taking the smallest steps toward healthier food choices can boost your energy and metabolism.
- Take time to pray, meditate and get back in touch with yourself. Slow down. Realign your inner thoughts. Be thankful. Be positive. Breathe.
- Give yourself positive affirmations and feedback. Speak your dreams into reality. Articulate your truth.

Avoid the Pitfalls

Ladies, let me forewarn you. When you share your dreams with others and seek like-minded people to expand your knowledge base, there will be a lot of untrustworthy people—and companies—who will tug at your emotional heartstrings. They will bombard your social media newsfeed and send emails repeatedly telling you to purchase their program and quit your job TODAY! You will receive emails from unknown individuals promoting the secrets of success and selling the "hidden keys" to achieving your dreams... if you simply invest in their program for a significant amount of money. You'll be invited to attend a three-day seminar that will immediately "Change Your Life." You'll receive work-from-home scams trying to lure you into starting a business with no investment. My advice to you is to hold off on investing in programs and seminars that promise you incredible results in a very short period of time. If it's too good to be true, then it's a scam.

By the way, these pitfalls aren't always monetary in nature. Often the pitfall is nothing more than a myth—something based in unreality that nevertheless sounds good enough to tempt you. You will find mythical stories and blogs about pursuing your passion that have been shared and re-shared on social media throughout the years. These stories highlight individual experiences of people like you who quit their jobs and found success pursuing their passion. Don't get me wrong, this can and does happen. However, this outcome is not the norm. The results simply aren't typical and usually require additional monetary resources and commitment to achieve the desired results. Don't allow yourself to be lured by promotions and propaganda that tell you to:

- Quit your job in thirty days or less and travel
- Do what you love today and the money will follow
- Pursuing your passion equals immediate profits
- Becoming an entrepreneur means being your own boss
- Hard work always equals success

Be wise. Be vigilant. Others will want to capitalize on your dreams. Be the gatekeeper. Be your own watchdog. Guard your dreams from those who will try to exploit or manipulate you. Then as you master your personal power and share your vision for your life, additional opportunities will happen, most likely without the requirement of monetary investments.

On my journey to lead the life I want after forty, I was exposed to all of the pitfalls listed above and more. The key to making the best decisions on your journey is to do your homework. Just because it sounds good doesn't mean it's good for you.

As always, consider the opportunity cost. What are you giving up to take advantage of this opportunity? Does the cost outweigh the benefit? Avoid making emotional decisions. Don't make important decisions when your frustrated, angry, or feeling overwhelmed. Let a clearer head prevail.

Defeat Procrastination

We've come full circle in this chapter. Again, it's time to get started! So if you find yourself endlessly tweaking your goals, perhaps you are overthinking the process. Building and defining goals can be complicated, but should not be a convoluted process. At this point, if you are so caught up in the minutia that you haven't yet started your journey, then you are very likely in "procrastination mode." Perhaps you feel a bit intimidated by the process. Perhaps you don't quite believe that you can do this.

Well ladies, the truth is that you are equipped and primed for the adventures ahead. You are intelligent and deserving and worthy of your dreams. You know where to start: with what matters most. Remember, you have the tools. Throughout these chapters you have learned how to let loose and dream, and then harness those dreams to goals. You have learned how to plan without online distractions. You have learned how to focus. Now all that is left is to get busy, and by "busy" I mean to walk through the process. You are ready to take the steps necessary to grow, bloom and prosper.

Let's evaluate. Below you'll recognize all the components necessary to be Fit, Fabulous and Focused.

FIT (Awareness)
Motivate Yourself. Stop Making Excuses
Find a Workout You Love
Learn to Say NO
Manage Your Emotions

FABULOUS (The Power of Choice)
Upgrade Your Perspective
Reinvent Yourself
Believe That You Can
Take Control of Your Finances
What about Love?

FOCUSED (Follow One Course Until Successful)
Create a Vision for Your Life
Adapt and Overcome
Assemble Your Dream Team
Ask for What You Really Want and Be Specific
Start Today

Follow the outline above. Refer to it often to unlock your potential and reach new heights. Better yet, re-read this book and highlight your favorite passages. Dog ear those pages, ladies! And if a pearl of wisdom strikes a chord, then hold it close to your heart and take action!

You, too, can be Fit, Fabulous and Focused after forty!

Bonus Chapter
30-Day Challenges

reating and managing change in your life is often easier said than done. In all honesty, it can actually be quite difficult! Despite your deepest desire to create or manage change, you may not have the discipline, direction or motivation it takes to make it happen. I understand and I was once in those same shoes. Maybe you've already read other books or watched videos about changing your life and still struggle with the day-to-day minutiae of how to make it happen. Perhaps you know *where* to begin but run short on momentum once you've gotten the ball rolling.

Those kinds of hurdles are exactly what the 30-day challenges at the end of the chapters in this book are designed to help you overcome. Each challenge provides the tools you desire to create and manage change in your life along with the framework you need to become disciplined and motivated throughout your journey. I help you figure it out so that you don't have to do it alone. Take advantage of the 30-day challenges in this self-help guide by using them as your personal tools to build your own Fit, Fabulous and Focused blueprint.

Don't spend another minute stuck in a rut or spinning your wheels being overwhelmed by the process. Let me show you how.

As a bonus to you in this ingenious self-help guide, I've combined all of the 30-day challenges from each chapter to serve as a quick reference toolkit. Refer to the challenges daily and use them often. Infuse them into your life to inspire change within yourself and to motivate others around you.

I'm so excited you've chosen my book as your personal resource to becoming Fit, Fabulous and Focused. If you don't complete a challenge within 30-days, that's okay. Take it as a learning experience and tweak your process before taking the next challenge; or repeat the same challenge until you complete it successfully. If you still need a little more encouragement as you complete your challenges, email me at info@fitfabfocus.com

Best of Luck!

Your Fit, Fabulous and Focused lifestyle awaits you

Yolanda

Fit Challenges

30-Day Motivational Challenges

'm happy to recommend some tried-and-true formulas that will help get your head back in the game. Try one or all of these 30-day challenges and you'll be up and moving in no time!

Become a Morning Person 30-Day Challenge:

- Set your clock to wake up 30 minutes to one hour earlier than usual.
- Go to bed earlier than your usual time. Try 9:30 or 10:00pm.
- Don't press snooze. Get up when the alarm rings the first time.

Minimize Distractions 30-Day Challenge (Take a "Media Fast"):

- Give up TV and stop following the news.
- Don't use the Internet for anything virtual for 30 days. No online banking, no social media, no Pandora, no You Tube, no CNN, no Netflix, or Hulu for 30 days.
- Check your email once per day unless it's work related.

Prioritize Your Goals 30-Day Challenge:

- Write at least one goal you'd like to accomplish on a piece of paper within the next 30 days. It can be personal or professional.

- Stick your goal on the mirror and say it out loud every morning when you wake up and every night before bed for the next 30 days.
- Dedicate at least 45 (uninterrupted) minutes per day to an activity that will help you achieve your goal.

30-Day Breakfast Challenge:

- Eat a nutritious breakfast every day for 30 days.
- Avoid doughnuts and other pastries for breakfast.
- Don't consume coffee and sodas as a supplement for a nutritional breakfast.

30-Day Workout Challenges

Imitation is the highest form of flattery, right? And if imitation can help you conquer new goals, then by all means identify your role model and follow her example!

The following 30-Day challenges for working out will propel you closer to what you personally envision.

30-Day Plank Challenge:

- The 30-day plank challenge only has one exercise which you have to do each day.
- Slowly build up your strength and core muscles by increasing the length of time each day.
- Gradually increase the time of your exercise until you reach a goal predetermined by you. (i.e. hold it for 60 seconds or 90 seconds).

30-Day Little Black Dress Challenge:

- Work on toning up a part of your body for thirty days. It can be your butt, abs, legs, arms, etc.
- After thirty days, put on your favorite little black dress and accentuate the body part you worked on during the thirty day period.

30-Day Hydrate your Body Challenge:

- Drink water and only water for thirty days. You may not get to eight glasses per day, but you must drink water for thirty days.
- No caffeine, no sodas, no coffee, or juices. Only water.
- Try to increase your water intake each day. You cannot drink less water than you did the previous day.

30-Day Get Outside Challenge:

- Take a break from the computer, the iPhone, the tablet and all of your other electronic gadgets.

- Every day, at least once a day, spend 20 minutes outside and take in some fresh air.
- Sit on the porch/deck.
- Walk the dog.
- Blow leaves or snow off the driveway.
- Water the flowers.
- Go for a walk.
- Ride a bike.

30-Day Challenges- Learn to Say "NO"

Whether it's family, church, friends, or self-defeating behaviors, learning to say NO is essential to building healthy relationships, establishing boundaries and creating a solid foundation for the life you want after forty. But learning to say NO doesn't happen overnight. You have to retrain your brain. Try your hand at a few of these 30-day challenges to kick-start your quest to say NO.

Quit a Bad Habit for 30 Days (to yourself):

- Give up games on your smart phone, eating fast food everyday, nail biting, smoking cigarettes, recreational drugs, eating sweets everyday, drinking alcohol excessively, or too much caffeine.
- Challenge yourself to kick at least one of those bad habits for thirty days.

No Apologies 30-day Challenge:

- Don't feel guilty after saying NO. Don't change your mind and cave in later.
- Don't apologize or offer excuses for saying NO.
- Do not be deceitful or lie.

30-Day Set Boundaries and Limitations Challenge (to others):

- For the next thirty days, whenever you say NO but feel guilty, write down all of the things you are saying YES to.
- Spend more quality time with family and friends.
- Take time to do things you like (i.e. hobbies).
- Enjoy having a reasonable and manageable workload.
- Appreciate the relaxation and peace of mind.

30-Day Emotional Challenges

Are you ready to be challenged? From time to time we all get a little emotional, so experiment with one (or all) of the challenges below to help curtail your emotional lows. It will help you better understand yourself and your triggers.

Manage Your Emotions for 30 Days:

- Don't raise your voice to get your point across.
- Don't yell or argue during conversations. Communicate in a normal tone with your kids, spouse, coworkers, colleagues, friends, etc.
- Maintain your composure. Find less aggressive ways to communicate to others.

No Complaining for 30 Days:

- Challenge yourself to be complaint free.
- No complaining about your job, your mate, your children, or your social life.
- No complaining about someone else's job, mate, children, or social life.

Keep a Gratitude Journal for 30 Days:

- Write something every day in your journal about why you are grateful.
- Do a little soul searching, count your blessings each day, and journalize your thoughts.

Potty Mouth Challenge (No Cursing for 30 Days):

- Stop swearing.
- Set a monetary amount to put in a jar each time you swear. It needs to be at least fifty cents per word.
- At the end of the month, donate the proceeds to someone in need or to a charitable cause.
- Stop and do 25 sit-ups or 15 push-ups each time you swear.

Fabulous Challenges

30-Day Challenges - Upgrading your Perspective

Changing the way you think or seeing things from a different point of view can be difficult but it is essential to your personal growth and development. Try these 30-day challenges below to start the process of upgrading your perspective. Remember, the change you seek starts from within.

30-Day Self-love Challenge:

- Write at least one positive thought about yourself every day for the next 30 days.
- Make the positive thought exclusive of your job, career title, or material possessions you own. The thought should be about you as a person and as a woman.
- The thought can be simple or complex, but it has to about you.

Ex: I am very compassionate and loving.
   I have a beautiful smile.
   I love my positive outlook on life.

30-Day Love Thy Neighbor Challenge:

- Buy a box of Thank You cards or blank cards.
- Every day for the next thirty days, write one compliment or nice thought about someone else.

- It can be your neighbor, friend, significant other, child, parent, etc.
- It has to a different person every day for the next thirty days.

Ex: My husband is very compassionate and loving.
My sister has a beautiful smile.
I love my coworker's positive outlook on life.

30-Day Challenges - Reinvent Yourself

Reinventing yourself can be a fun and rewarding experience. Let the 30-day challenges below help you change the way you see yourself and move beyond your comfort zone.

30-Day Clean up the Clutter Challenge:

- For the next thirty days, spend time making your home happy by removing clutter.
- Spend thirty days clearing out anything that you have not used within the past three months.
- Discard or shred any magazines, receipts, medicine, food, and vitamins that are beyond their expiration date.
- Donate any clothes, make-up, perfume, jewelry, old electronics, and shoes that you have not worn or used with the past two years.
- If you can't declutter your home in 30 days, break the task into areas such as the bedroom, the kitchen, and the family room. Tackle one area every 30 days.

30-Day Recycle Your Wardrobe:

- Choose ten outfits from your current wardrobe. Challenge yourself to make each outfit noticeably different the next time you wear it.
- You may use your current earrings, purses, shoes, leggings, hats, hosiery, scarves, jewelry, nail polish, makeup, and hair accessories to accentuate the outfit.
- You must wear the recycled outfits again within the thirty-day period.

30-Day Embrace New Technology Challenge:

- Identify one aspect of technology or social networking that you do not use (i.e. Bluetooth, Talk to text, Instagram, Twitter, etc.).
- Use it avidly for the next thirty days.

30-Day Gain a New Skill to Add to your Resume:

- Attend a continuing education class, seminar, or on-the-job cross-training opportunity within the next thirty days.
- Thoroughly familiarize yourself with this new skill during a thirty-day period.
- Add the new skill to your resume.

30-Day Challenges - Believe that You Can

With so much going on in your daily routine, it's easy to unknowingly incorporate doubt an uncertainty into your psyche. Try the 30-day challenges below to redirect the negative energy you encounter throughout your day.

30-Day Negativity Fast:

- Avoid words with contractions for 30 Days.
- Remove words like don't, can't, won't and shouldn't from your vocabulary for 30 days.
- Rephrase your thoughts to convey the same response without using negative contractions.
- Instead of saying "I don't want to go," try saying "I would prefer to pass at the moment."

30-Day Visualize your Success Challenge:

- Spend at least 30 minutes every day visualizing your success at something you want to achieve.
- Imagine every aspect of your success as if it was your 15 minutes of fame.
- Get lost in the moment and utilize all of your senses.
- Imagine what that glorious moment will feel like, what kind of day it will arrive on, what will you wear, who will be around, and what sounds you will hear in the background.
- Write down those thoughts every day.

30-Day Positivity Challenge:

- For the next 30 days, try to only think positive thoughts and focus on a positive outlook.
- Whatever happens, you will see the good side and discover positive "take aways."
- No criticism, complaining, or negative commentary can be spoken aloud for 30 straight days.

30-Day Challenges - Financial Freedom

Ladies, you can improve your financial fitness by maintaining your focus and making smart financial moves. The 30-day challenges below can help!

30-Day Fiscal Fast (A No-Spend Month)

- Plan ahead for your fiscal fast and sit tight during the tempting holiday months.
- Don't buy anything that isn't necessary to live for thirty days. If it isn't food, medicine, or gas for your car, don't buy it.
- Take your lunch to work. Cook breakfast and dinner. Eat meals at home on the weekends and go out for activities in between meals.
- No debit or credit cards or online spending. No impulse spending.
- Track your lessons learned and changes you'd like to make.

30-Day Challenge: Set the Record Straight

- Over the next thirty days, take a look at all of your current insurance policies, your Will, investment accounts, etc.
- Update your beneficiary information, distributions, and instructions.
- Print a copy of all documentation and put it in a safe, accessible place.

Focused Challenges

30-Day Challenges - Create a Vision for your Life

Life happens and often times we get inundated with our daily grind—so inundated that we go for weeks, months, even years without dreaming BIG. There are some people who don't dream at all. Take a break from your day-to-day activities and find time to dream again. The thirty day challenges below will help you get started.

30-Day Create a Vision Board and Action Plan

- Spend a day or a weekend on Pinterest and other sites planning your vision board.
- Gather your ideas and create a vision board.
- Spend no less than thirty minutes each time you work on your board throughout over the next thirty days.
- Share your vision board with at least one important person in your life on the thirtieth day.

30-Day Dream BIG Challenge

- On the first day, write down one dream that you have and would like to pursue.
- Day two—add something additional to your dream. For example, if you dream of buying a five bedroom, five bath home on day one, then add a swimming pool and a gardener on day two. On

day three, make it a beach house at your favorite vacation spot. Day four, make the dream bigger. You can make it as lavish or exciting or imaginative as you want.

- By day thirty, go back and read what you added each day to your original dream. See how much you allowed your mind to stretch beyond your original dream.
- If the dream was too small, repeat the process.

30-Day Challenges - Assemble Your Dream Team

Nurture your team and help your team members shine! The challenges below can help you be the leader your team needs and deserves.

30-Day Challenge: Organize your Team Base

- Clear out old emails. If you need them for future reference, store them on the cloud or on an external drive for safe keeping.
- Get rid of old contacts from your phone.
- Delete old text messages from your mobile devices.
- Encourage your team to do the same so they can become organized and efficient.

30-Day Challenge: Find a Mentor

- Google the Chamber of Commerce and local business clubs to identify movers and shakers within your community.
- Don't overlook the wise old souls who know a lot about human relations and real world experiences. Research retired professors, business leaders and society mavens who know what it takes to become successful.
- Reach out—don't be shy! Chances are, someone will feel honored to become your mentor.

30-Day Challenge: Connect Outside of Social Media

- Go where the action is. Attend meetings and networking groups. Seek out social activities that require face-to-face interaction.
- Join a walking group, a breakfast club, or a class at church.
- Consider a speed dating adventure and get to know a multitude of people in mere seconds!
- Strike up conversations at the bookstore, the local coffee shop, the gym or the park.
- Become empowered through conversation and friendly discourse.

30-Day Challenge: Start a Meet Up Group in Your City

- Join a meet-up group by and for aficionados in your same field. Soak up their wisdom while socializing.
- Better yet, start your own group and attract like-minded people who enjoy sharing their own dreams, visions and goals.
- If you have more than one passion, join or start several meet-up groups and revel in the authenticity of personal connections.

30-Day Challenges —Ask for What You Want

Build courage and confidence by asking for what you want. The 30-Day challenges below can help you ask for what you really want in specific terms.

30-Day Challenge: Become a Better Speaker

- Try not to use "uh" or "mmm" while speaking publicly.
- If you are speaking to an audience and feel an "uh" or "mmm" coming on, take a breather. Pause or slow down and take a moment to collect your thoughts.
- Practice speaking publicly before an event. Practice makes perfect.

30-Day Challenge: The Discount Challenge

- Choose a restaurant or retailer and purchase an item.
- Ask for a 10% discount with no rhyme or reason.
- Repeat the process daily over the thirty day period.

30-Day Challenge: Ask for it Challenge

- Spend thirty days asking for things you want or need.
- Find something new to ask for every day
  - Help with a project/chore
  - Information
  - Perks
  - Directions
  - Feedback
  - Favors
  - Raises
  - Discounts
  - Love/Sex
  - Attention
  - More Paid Time Off
  - More Quality Time
  - More Romance
  - Financial Assistance

About the Author

What began as a hobby of writing pocket-sized "How To" fitness guides for Divas to sell at local gyms and fitness studios in her hometown, Macon, GA, has slowly evolved into a passion for writing self-help books for women. As a former fitness studio owner, Yolanda Cornelius, cleverly repurposed her former business concept, Diva Zone Studios, and opened her own publishing company, Diva Zone Publishing. She self-published her first book "Pocket-guide to Pole Dancing" in 2015 under the pseudonym Definitely Diva and recently completed her second book "Fit, Fabulous and Focused. How to Create the Life You Want after Forty". Yolanda plans to continue writing a series of self-help books for women and also incorporating the pocket-guides for divas into future projects.